Cultural Inclusion: The Case of Persons with Disabilities in Jamaica

FLOYD MORRIS

RESOURCE *Publications* • Eugene, Oregon

Arawak publications
Kingston • Jamaica

26 25 24 23 22
e   d   c   b   a

Information received from personal communication or from elite interviews with
the researcher/author has been reproduced by kind courtesy of the interviewees
and those who shared personal information. It is therefore with sincere gratitude
and deep respect that the author gives full credit to these persons for their selfless
contributions.

NATIONAL LIBRARY OF JAMAICA CATALOGUING-IN-PUBLICATION DATA

Name: Morris, Floyd, author.
Title: Cultural inclusion : the case of persons with disabilities in
   Jamaica / Floyd Morris.
Description: Kingston : Arawak publications, 2022.
Subjects: LCSH: Disabilities and popular music – Jamaica. | Musicians
   with disabilities – Jamaica. | Popular culture – Jamaica.
Classification: DDC 781.64087 -- dc23.

This edition licensed by special permission of Arawak publications

Resource Publications
An Imprint of Wipf and Stock Publishers
199 W. 8th Ave, Suite 3
Eugene, OR 97401

www.wipfandstock.com

ISBN: 978-1-6667-4168-1 (paperback)
ISBN: 978-1-6667-4169-8 (hardcover)
ISBN: 978-1-6667-4170-4 (eBook)

Book & cover design by Annika Lewinson-Morgan

Set in Iowan Old Style 10.5/13pt with Hoefler Text

Contents

Dedication

This book is dedicated to the community of persons
with disabilities in Jamaica.
These are individuals who have been marginalized
and discriminated against in the society
due to circumstances beyond their control.
This has served to stymie the talents and abilities
of thousands of Jamaicans, all on the basis of their disability.
Those, such as the subjects of this book,
who have disabilities have yet challenged the system,
have managed to overcome the restrictions in the society
and have served as examples to all.
Persons with disabilities can be justly proud
of their unassailable contribution
to the development of Jamaica's culture.

Acknowledgements

I wish to express my profound appreciation to a number of individuals who offered selfless assistance and support for the research which led to this book. Without their contribution and invaluable input, the project would be meaningless.

First, I must extend profound appreciation to Mr Jason Ricketts and Mr Shavane Daley for their Herculean efforts to collect and collate the data for the research. Their dedication and commitment to the process are profoundly appreciated. As Research Assistants on the project, both Jason and Shavane were engaged to collect the data and assist in preparing some of the chapters of this book. Credit is hereby given to them for their tremendous role.

I wish to express profound appreciation to all the persons whose experiences are documented here – alive or deceased. Without their sterling contribution to the culture, there would be nothing to document. Persons with disabilities, including myself, can be justly proud of their involvement in Jamaica's development through entertainment and music.

Full appreciation must be given to The University of the West Indies for its support. It continues to be a beacon in advancing the development trajectory of persons with disabilities.

I must express my sincere appreciation to God for continued guidance and direction in my life. It is from His guidance and lead that I developed the knowledge and understanding necessary for preparing this book.

Introduction

Culture is extremely important to the development of any society (Higman 2004). It addresses the values and practices within a community that make it unique and distinct. It forms that identifying and distinguishing mark of a people, and being immeasurable, it is a concept which makes its definition problematic for researchers. Jamaica's unique, world recognized culture is best manifested in its language, food and music. With entertainment and music playing pivotal roles, diverse individuals have contributed to the development and shaping of this sector, and efforts have been made to document the input of these artistes. The works of Niaah 2020, Hope 2013, Howard 2007, Cooper 2004, and Stolzoff 2002, for example, attest to this. However, in the chronicling of these narratives, the impact of persons with disabilities has not been sufficiently captured. It is within this context that this book was written.

Jamaica is known to the world for its strong musical mastery. Different people have contributed to this, and scholars have sought to document the narratives of these contributors. Niaah (2020), Hope (2015, 2018), Howard (2007, 2016) and Cooper (2004) are the scholars who have played a leading role in chronicling the contribution of popular music to the development of Jamaica's culture.

Hope, for example, in one of her outstanding academic pieces, *Reggae Stories: Jamaican Musical Legends and Cultural Legacies* (2018), makes a colossal effort to document the contribution of various Jamaican artistes to the development of Jamaica's culture. Niaah, through her work *Dancehall: A Reader on Jamaican Music and Culture* (2020), highlights the impact of dancehall on the cultural formation of Jamaica. Cooper in *Sound Clash: Jamaican Dancehall Culture at Large* (2004) makes an exceptional contribution to the documentation of popular music in Jamaica's culture. Similarly, Howard in his insightful book, *The Creative Echo Chamber:*

Contemporary Music Production in Kingston, Jamaica (2016), does a marvellous job in chronicling the unique contribution of popular music to Jamaica's culture.

However, a gap exists in these chronicles as it relates to persons with disabilities who have received minimal focus, although they have been major contributors. In fact, there has been no substantive work which documents the contribution of these persons to culture in Jamaica or the Caribbean. Conspicuously, most of the available literature chronicling the contribution of persons with disabilities to Jamaican culture through music and entertainment has been done through magazines or newspapers – for example, the *Jamaica Gleaner* and *Jamaica Observer*. This book therefore attempts to record their contribution, through musical inclusion and participation, to the cultural development of Jamaica.

Jamaica has developed its own variety of music that has garnered world attention (Stolzoff 2002; Prahlad 2001). This music, reggae, has featured prominently in the halls of some kings and queens across the globe. Freedom fighters worldwide have used it as motivational music – for example, in African states such as Zimbabwe, South Africa, Angola, and others, between the 1960s and 1990s. Wherever you take it, reggae has been a major selling point for Jamaica, as the world danced and sang to the music of stars such as Bob Marley, Jimmy Cliff, Sean Paul, and Shaggy, to name a few (Hope 2015). Their chants and lyrics alongside the pulsating reggae beat have won admiration and respect throughout the world for a country with a population of just 2.7 million inhabitants.

The colossal efforts of Jamaicans to create and market their unique product have not gone unnoticed. In 2018 UNESCO declared Jamaica as the origin and home of reggae music (Rolling Stone 2018). This international affirmation has given the country global recognition and protection of a product created solely by Jamaicans.

Non-disabled citizens are not exclusively responsible for Jamaica's musical development and cultural formation; persons with disabilities have also made immense contributions, especially in the area of Jamaican popular music. Individuals such as Frankie Paul, Derrick Morgan, Roy Richards, along with bands such as Fab Five and Unique Vision have all made stellar contributions to the Jamaican music industry. Fab Five is currently one of the oldest musical bands in the island, having been around for over 50 years. The band has contributed to diverse aspects of the music, in distinct musical spaces and genres such as in festivals and dance halls, and with soca or ska in addition to reggae. Fab Five has been a consistent staple in the popular musical development of the country.

Persons with disabilities have used music as a means of expressing their talents over the years (Howe et al. 2015; Straus 2011). It is one of the more inclusive areas in the society where they have been allowed to participate, albeit while being viewed as playing a less dominant role. Nevertheless, their participation has been characterized by excellence as they demonstrate that they can perform as well as their non-disabled counterparts.

Internationally, prominent persons with disabilities such as Beethoven, Fanny Crosby, Stevie Wonder, and Ray Charles have dominated the musical arena. All have displayed musical excellence and their music continues to be played in opera houses, the media, churches, clubs and at large social gatherings. Their music has positively impacted the lives of all people.

Nationally, the strong participation of individuals already mentioned and others like Adina Edwards are evident in the music industry. Similar to the international icons named earlier, their music too has been featured strongly in playhouses or theatres, churches, the media, clubs, dance halls and major national festival activities. Wherever they play or sing, people are stimulated.

The fundamental question by scholars and lay persons might be, "What makes these persons with disabilities excel in the field of music?" Various responses have been offered. Some argue that the disability requires that they focus more on their task and this attitude contributes to their excellence. Others say that it is simply because they are gifted. Another school of thought posits that the loss of one biological sense heightens the others, and this allows persons with a disability to deal with musical instruments in a way non-disabled persons cannot. While the arguments may all contain elements of truth, the overarching assertion is that persons with disabilities have made astounding contributions to musical developments across the world. Straus' seminal work, *Extraordinary Measures: Disability in Music* (2011), for example, captures the impact of disability and concepts of disability on composers, performers and listeners with disabilities as well as discussions on music and works of music. This extraordinary scholarly work by Straus, however, documented by and large a Eurocentric version of the contribution of individuals with disabilities to music.

Despite the progress made by persons with disabilities in music, there has been limited research on their contribution to the cultural environment of Jamaica. The need for this has been recognized, and has prompted a major study, the findings of which are presented here.

The Theoretical Framework

In conducting this assessment of the contribution of persons with disabilities to the development of Jamaica's culture, two theoretical frames are used to anchor the arguments. These are social constructionism and social cognitive theory (SCT).

Berger and Luckmann in their seminal book *The Social Construction of Reality* (1966) posited that society is created by humans and human interactions which are regarded as habitualization. This is the process by which any frequently repeated action becomes a pattern which can then be performed again in the future in the same manner and with the same economical effort (Berger and Luckmann 1966). It is this repeated action that gives meaning to objects and things in society.

According to Mitcham and Ryder (2005), social constructionism concerns the meaning, notion or connotation placed on an object or event by society and adopted by the members of that society based on how they relate to or deal with the object or event. Individuals formulate meaning based on their socialization and relate to things and individuals based on their lived reality.

Social constructionism has direct implications for understanding persons with disabilities, because it is individuals in society that determine, through the multiple barriers they place in the way of persons with impairments, how these individuals are included and perceived in society. To this end, we turn to Mike Oliver's (1990) social model of disability for a better understanding. In this context, Oliver postulates that:

1. Impairment is lacking part of or all of a limb or having a defective limb, organism or mechanism of the body;
2. Disability is the disadvantage or restriction of activity caused by a contemporary social organization which takes no or little account of people who have physical impairments and thus excludes them from the mainstream of social activities (Oliver 1990: 33–34).

Here we see Oliver making a distinction between impairment and disability. Impairment is the physical condition affecting the individual. However, when the person with the impairment interacts with society, that is where, according to Oliver, the disability comes into play.

It is individuals in society that set the inclusion or exclusion criteria for knowledge and understanding of a society. Invariably, persons with disabilities are restricted due to the diverse barriers that are placed in their pathway by non-disabled individuals. In the context of this book, it is reflected in the exclusion of these individuals from the academic literature where the contribution to Jamaica's culture is concerned. There is no academic literature on the cultural contribution of persons with disabilities in Jamaica. Persons with disabilities who are in the academic space must therefore correct this exclusion.

SCT was developed by Albert Bandura (1986) and posits that portions of an individual's knowledge attainment can be related to observing others within the context of social interactions, experiences and outside media influences. Bandura specifically argues that human behaviour is caused by personal, behavioural and environmental factors (Bandura 1986).

Through a schematic presentation, Bandura highlights how the reproduction of observed behaviour is inspired by a three-dimensional interaction, namely:

1. **Personal** – referring to whether or not the individual has high or low self-efficacy towards the behaviour. One must get the individual to believe in his or her personal abilities to effectively complete the behaviour.
2. **Behavioural** – referring to the response that an individual receives subject to completing a behaviour. One must provide opportunities for the individual to experience success consequent to performing the behaviour correctly.
3. **Environmental** – referring to environmental factors that influence the individual's ability to complete a behaviour successfully. This entails the provision of appropriate support and materials for improved self-efficacy (Bandura 1986).

Admittedly, this researcher's knowledge and understanding of persons with disabilities has come about due to personal experience, years of interaction with members of this marginalized community, and extensive research conducted (Morris 2017). The arguments posited by Bandura (1986) are linked to those of Oliver (1990) and are confirmed by this author's observations over the years of interaction with the community of persons with disabilities in Jamaica. For example, the environmental factors are not constructed for persons with disabilities to be included in mainstream society and enjoy success in whatsoever they are required to do. Furthermore, when most of these marginalized citizens participate in an activity, society is not expecting them to succeed because of the way they are perceived by the broader society. This is why their contribution to the development of society is not captured in any significant way in academic literature in the region, and efforts must be made to correct this deficit.

Contextually, therefore, the two theories mentioned (social constructionism and social cognitive theory) are conflated to give the quintessence of the arguments being presented in this book. In the chronicling of the contribution of persons with disabilities to the development of Jamaica's culture, note has to be taken of their experience with the varied barriers that have been used to restrict the participation and inclusion of these marginalized citizens in the broader society. When persons with disabilities do get the opportunity to participate, their level of efficacy is not treated as significant because individuals within society have formulated perceptions as to how successful they can be. Persons with disabilities therefore have to work doubly hard to be successful in order to meet the inclusion criteria set by non-disabled individuals in society.

Methodology

Guided by an interpretivist paradigm, a qualitative approach was used to capture data from individuals involved; and in order to give real meaning and understanding to the cultural development of Jamaica, the contributions of key stakeholders – persons with disabilities – have been documented. The interpretivist paradigm embraces qualitative methodology. An intimate understanding of the subjects was therefore acquired through interviews, observations and experiences, in order to accurately interpret the language that is used. Case studies, elite interviews, and documentary interrogations were the major approaches employed in documenting and showcasing how persons with disabilities have added value to the Jamaican culture through their entertainment and musical contributions, and to demonstrate the success of their careers. Their experiences present possibilities for talented persons with disabilities to forge viable career paths.

In the case studies presented, attention is placed on the origins of the individual or band, the source of inspiration; experiences; failures and successes; lessons learnt and recommendations for action. A series of elite interviews was also conducted with key stakeholders such as sound system operators, radio broadcasters, promoters, managers and producers who worked with these artists to gain in-depth knowledge of the work of the subject and also for triangulation. All the interviews were conducted between June and November 2017. Questionnaires were employed and responses were captured on digital tape and transcribed into print for further collation and analysis.

Secondary data was collected from various archiving sources which proved invaluable to the gathering of information for this book. These included the *Gleaner, Jamaica Observer*, Radio Jamaica, the Public Broadcasting Corporation of Jamaica (PBCJ), the Jamaica Information Service (JIS), the Institute of Jamaica (IOJ), and the Jamaica Library Service (JLS).

Chapter 1 gives a contextual framework of the situation of persons with disabilities in Jamaica. In chapters 2–12 of the book, case studies of individuals or groups are presented. In chapter 2, the focus is on Don Drummond who, despite his mental illness, was one of the most outstanding trombonists the island has ever seen. In chapter 3, the focus is on Michael "Askhelle" Fairman who was a visually impaired reputed king of beats. "Israel Vibration" was a dynamic trio that provided Jamaica with pulsating reggae music whose members were stricken by the poliovirus which attacks the spinal cord and causes paralysis. Their journey is chronicled in chapter 4.

In chapter 5, we look at the life of the blind Damion Rose, professionally known as "DJ Cane", a disc jockey and audio sound engineer living and operating out of Kingston, Jamaica. Derrick Morgan, one of the legends in the music industry in Jamaica, who is also visually impaired, is featured in chapter 6. The "Certified Diva" Latifa Brown, who was born with a growth disorder that affects the bones of the lower limbs is at the centre of chapter 7, while chapter 8 features Peter Clarke and Devon Palmer, blind masters at musical instruments.

Chapter 9 salutes Frankie Paul, the "Tu-Sheng-Peng" general who is visually impaired, as is Dwayne Hamilton, the master dancehall selector who is the centre of attention in chapter 10. The "Jewel" of Jamaica's roots rocking reggae bands, the "Fabulous Five" or "Fab Five", in which two of its three founders were visually impaired, is highlighted in chapter 11. In chapter 12, we focus on the contribution of Adina Edwards, an outstanding gospel artist who was blind.

Chapter 13 presents a summation of the findings, analysis and recommendations for action. In this connection, the author's Afterword entitled "Seismic Shift for Persons with Disabilities in Jamaica" (reproduced from his 20 February 2022 contribution to *The Gleaner*) celebrates "the coming into effect" of the Disabilities Act on 14 February 2022 as "one of the most far-reaching pieces of social legislation to be implemented in the country".

Where people are quoted directly, unless otherwise indicated, the quotes are from personal communication with the researcher or from elite interviews. For ethical reasons, no attempt has been made to modify or translate their language, which is more often than not in Jamaican (Jamaican Creole).

The academic community should find this work invaluable as it presents new documentation of facts and new perspectives. It should also be of interest to music aficionados, historians and citizens who appreciate good music, as well as to members of the community of persons with disabilities.

It should be noted that author and lead researcher Floyd Morris as well as research assistants Jason Ricketts and Shavane Daley are all blind. This gives true meaning to the global mantra of persons with disabilities: "Nothing About Us Without Us" (Crowther 2007). Furthermore, the personal experiences of these individuals do contribute to an understanding of the subject under study as postulated by Bandura (1986).

Morris has been a passionate advocate for persons with disabilities and, as a qualitative researcher, his intimate connection to the subject could impact the interpretation and analysis of the data. Additionally, as he is also friends with some of the individuals who are featured in the case studies, the inclusion of secondary data sources was used to substantiate claims, thus ensuring the validity and credibility of the central arguments presented in this work.

Contextualizing the Situation of Persons with Disabilities in Jamaica

"I want to remind the members of this Honourable Chamber and the broader public that disability respects no one as you can be fully abled today and disabled tomorrow. We therefore have to respect these individuals and treat them the way we would want to be treated if we should develop a disabling condition. Disability is not restrictive to a particular set of individuals; it can happen to any of us. Give them reasonable opportunities to participate in the society."

(Morris 2018)

The above statement is an extract from a debate in the Jamaican Senate in May 2018 on the new Road Traffic Act. It is a perspicuous reminder that disability respects no one and can happen at any time. It is therefore incumbent on individuals in society to create mechanisms for these marginalized individuals to be included and participate in society on an equal basis with others.

In this chapter, the author contextualizes the situation of persons with disabilities in Jamaica. One has to be reminded of the socio-cultural environment in which they operate and in spite of this, manage to make a meaningful contribution to the development of their society. Disability, we understand from Mike Oliver, comes about when an individual with an impairment interacts with various social factors in society and these factors restrict their equal participation with others in society (Oliver 1990). The United Nations Convention on the Rights of Persons with Disabilities (CRPD) regards persons with disabilities as "those individuals who have long-term physical, mental, intellectual or sensory impairments which in interaction with various barriers may hinder their full and effective participation in society on an equal basis with others" (United Nations 2006: 4).

Persons with disabilities are among the most marginalized in any society (World Health Organization 2011). Their marginality is due to their having lower health outcomes, least likely to access quality education, lower participation in the labour market, and negative attitudes and stigma from individuals in society. All of these contribute to persons with disabilities being among the poorest in society, and this is reinforced by various barriers that they have to confront on a daily basis.

Barriers to Persons with Impairment

There are many barriers that persons with impairment have to confront in the Jamaican society. However, for the purpose of this book, focus will be placed on five of them in order to give readers a vivid understanding of the environment in which the subjects have to operate. These five barriers are: access to education; access to employment; access to public facilities; access to information; and negative attitudes and stigma.

Education

Education, an indispensable right for persons with disabilities (Rieser 2008), is often restricted due to extensive inaccessibility to educational institutions (United Nations 2018). Studies of the Jamaican education system have suggested that most of the schools are inaccessible to these students (Morris 2010). A 2018 report on the situation of children with disabilities in Jamaica reveals that:

> Access to education remains a significant barrier to PWDs achieving their full potential. Though significant strides have been made in promoting inclusion and access, PWDs still do not possess educational levels that are on par with the wider population. The Census 2001 showed that the highest level of education attained by the majority of PWDs (41.8%) was primary level education. This was followed by 35.3% attaining secondary level education. In contrast, most persons without disabilities (47.8%) had attained a secondary level education, followed by 27.7% acquiring only a primary level education (UNICEF 2018: 21).

If the talents and abilities of these marginalized persons are to be maximized, then they have to have greater access to and inclusion in mainstream educational institutions (ECLAC 2017). As articulated by Bandura (1986), this is what is going to increase their efficacy.

When we speak of accessible and inclusive educational institutions, we are speaking about mechanisms where children with disabilities are allowed to participate in the same educational settings and institutions as children without disabilities (UNESCO 2009). For example, there should be access to the physical building housing the educational institution. Teachers should be trained in how to teach children with disabilities, and there should be modern technologies that would allow for easy interaction between children with disabilities and others in the educational institution (Rieser 2008).

Most of the people interviewed in this book attended special educational institutions, where children with disabilities are isolated from the mainstream (Gooden-Monteith 2019). It is here that they got exposure to music which paved the way for their contribution to national development. But it is felt by some scholars that special education robs persons with disabilities of their fundamental right to a high quality education (Rieser 2008). It can be argued that if the people described here had been included in mainstream educational institutions, they would have been better able to assist in changing some of the negative attitudes and stigma in the broader Jamaican society (Anderson 2014). Non-disabled students attending these institutions would have been exposed to their talents and abilities from an early stage, and based on this interaction and experience, would have had a more positive view of persons with disabilities (Bandura 1986).

Special education institutions emanated from the era of the welfare perspective of persons with disabilities. In this era, persons with disabilities were viewed and treated as charity cases (Anderson 2014) and as such, they were isolated from mainstream educational institutions. Special education institutions do not allow for persons with disabilities to maximize their full potential, nor do they allow these marginalized citizens to be brought into the mainstream of society (Rieser 2008). This is why the United Nations is advocating that as far as practicable, persons with disabilities should be included in the mainstream education systems (United Nations 2018).

Employment

Every human being has the right to work – including persons with disabilities (United Nations 2006, 1948). Notwithstanding this right, persons with disabilities have been excluded from the labour market in Jamaica and research data has suggested that up to 91.1 per cent of them are unemployed, with most of these individuals residing in rural Jamaica (MLSS 2015). This is why some have resorted to self-employment activities, and the music and entertainment industry presents viable options in this regard. However, the start-up capital required for these ventures can be extremely prohibitive and therefore only a few persons with disabilities get the opportunity to venture into this type of self-employment activity. Efforts must be put in place by the Government of Jamaica, as in jurisdictions such as Canada, the United States, the United Kingdom, Australia and New Zealand, to make persons with disabilities access equipment that will contribute to their own employment.

Access to Public Facilities

Access to public facilities is foundational to the inclusion and participation of persons with disabilities in the mainstream of society (Morris 2020). Without access to public facilities, these individuals will not be able to access services that will contribute to their growth and development on an equal basis with others in society. Article 9 of the CRPD affirms this right of persons with disabilities to access public facilities (United Nations 2006). In fact, the General Comments on Article 9 on Accessibility provided by the Committee on the Rights of Persons with Disabilities stipulates that the duty to provide accessibility is an *ex ante* duty. This means that accessibility must be provided before a person with a disability makes a request to use a place or service (Committee on the Rights of Persons with Disabilities 2014).

Accessing public facilities has been a significant challenge for persons with disabilities (Morris 2020). Most of the public facilities have been built without the requisite facilities to accommodate persons with disabilities, and this is more pronounced in rural Jamaica. Educational institutions, health facilities, parks, shopping facilities, work places, sidewalks, public transportation and other facilities have not been consistently built to include and allow for the participation of persons with disabilities in the island (Morris 2020).

It has thus taken a tenacious spirit, along with grit and determination for the subjects of this book to have accomplished what they have in their musical exploits. These men and women have had to traverse the country in buses and cars without any special accessibility features. They have had to dance around potholes and dangling wires on sidewalks. And, they have had to rock and roll with educational institutions that have limited or no access for persons with disabilities. This is the context in which these individuals have operated and achieved excellence. Can you imagine what would happen if there were a more accessible society for persons with disabilities? Access to public facilities is therefore a national imperative that must be realized if persons with disabilities are to be included in the mainstream of Jamaican society.

Access to Information

We are living in modern era where access to information is indispensable (Blumler and Cavanagh 1999). In the United Nations Convention on the Rights of Persons with Disabilities (CRPD), State Parties are mandated to ensure that persons with disabilities have access to information and in an accessible format (United Nations 2006). This means that information should be readily available in braille or large print for the blind and visually impaired; there should be the use of sign language and or closed-captioning for the deaf and hard of hearing; and the use of easy to read text for persons with intellectual disabilities. If information is not made available to persons with disabilities in an accessible format, these citizens will be excluded from participating in the mainstream of society. Inaccessibility to information has been the experience of members of this marginalized community in the Jamaican society for years, and this has stymied the contribution of this sector to national development.

Attitudes and Stigmas

Persons with disabilities have to work doubly hard to make their contribution to every aspect of Jamaican society. Years of negative socialization and stigma have contributed to these individuals being seen in a negative light (Morris 2017; Anderson 2014). It is what this author regards as "disability infodemics", as half-truths and false information are deeply entrenched in the Jamaican society about persons with disabilities. Some Jamaicans perceive these marginalized individuals as not being able to make a significant contribution, and deliberately isolate them from the development agenda. It is the perception of some that the best place for a person with a disability is in their home where they can rely on family and the state for support (Staniland 2011). A UNICEF-supported 2006 study reveals that some parents in Jamaica perceived the birth of their child with a disability as supernaturally connected. Forty per cent of parents perceived that the child was "sent by God", whilst 18 per cent thought the disability was "due to an evil spirit, punishment for a sin, or looking at a disabled person during pregnancy" (UNICEF 2006). Consequently, when persons with disabilities do get the opportunity to make their contribution, they are overshadowed by these myths and stigmas and therefore have to work even harder than the non-disabled to have their efforts recognized in Jamaica.

This is an important reason that persons with disabilities who are engaged in academic work must ensure that there is a chronicling of this sector's contribution to the society. It is within this context that this book has been written.

But to change these negative attitudes and stigmas towards persons with disabilities will require consistent public awareness campaigning (Bandura 2001). Years of negative socialization cannot be jettisoned overnight; eradicating this entirely will require deliberate, consistent and strategic effort on the part of all stakeholders (United Nations 2018, 2006). Importantly, individuals with disabilities, such as the subjects of this book who have been successful in their musical exploits, will have to play a lead role in transforming these negative attitudes and stigmas.

All of these barriers are socially constructed (Oliver 2013, 1990). For them to be eradicated and for increased efficacy for persons with disabilities in society, there must be greater understanding of how members of this community operate and function (Bandura 1986). Furthermore, there will have to be deliberate communicative action by government, and by non-governmental organizations catering to persons with disabilities, to transform the society to be more inclusive (Bandura 2001). Thankfully, we are seeing some attempts at this in Jamaica, as evidenced by the passage of the Disabilities Act 2014 (MLSS 2014) which when implemented will, inter alia, make it mandatory for measures to be put in place by different stakeholders in the society, to improve communication with persons with disabilities.

The Disabilities Act 2014 is a vital piece of legislation in changing the Jamaican landscape for persons with disabilities. For years, efforts at including persons with disabilities in the mainstream of society and allowing for their full and efficacious participation were hinged on moral suasion. This has not yielded the desired results and prompted the Government of Jamaica in 2014 to enact legislation to protect these marginalized individuals. However, some seven years after the legislation was passed in the Parliament, the authorities have failed to implement it. The cavalier manner in which the legislation has been treated is symptomatic of how persons with disabilities are perceived in the broader society and the priority given to matters relating to these marginalized citizens. As mentioned previously, when implemented, the legislation will provide for the inclusion and participation of persons with disabilities in some preeminent areas of Jamaican life. This will make it easier for persons with disabilities to realize their goals and aspirations in life and become major contributors to society as are the subjects of this book.

Don Drummond: Pre-eminent Jamaican Trombonist

(I'll never, I'll never...)
I'll never grow old
No, I'll never grow old
'Cause I walk and I walk
And I talk and I talk
I search... until I found my love.

(I'll never, I'll never, I'll never...)
I will never grow old
I'll never grow old
(I'll never, never, never, never, never...)
And I walk and I walk
And I talk and I talk
I search... until I found my love.

(Toots and the Maytals featuring Terry Hall and U-Roy
backed by the Skatalites 1963)

Don Drummond (March 12, 1932–May 6, 1969) is one of the best known persons in Jamaica with mental illness to have made a significant contribution to the music industry.

Arguably one of the best trombonists to have graced Jamaica in his short life, "Don D" Drummond profoundly impacted the Jamaican musical landscape and influenced the perception of the trombone. The trombone is a 15th century musical instrument and a member of the brass family. As with all brass instruments, the sound is produced by buzzing the lips into a mouthpiece. One unique feature of the trombone is the slide. While other brass instruments change pitch by pressing valves to change the length of the air flow, the trombone player simply moves the slide in and out to change the length of the instrument (*Encyclopaedia Britannica* 2018). "Some people didn't know his name. Others never saw him in person or seen him perform, but most people who were connected to any kind of music in Jamaica during the 1950s and 1960s would probably know about the best trombone player of that era" (Katz 2013).

Close friend and confidante, Winston Smith, believed that in his relatively short life Drummond achieved so much that it made him recognized as being among the best the world had ever seen:

> *There were not very many trombone players during that period. Of course there were men like Carl Masters, Von Muller (Mullo) and a few more that were there before Don came along; but none of them lit up the spotlight like he did. This man has been heard by a number of foreigners who gave laurels for his brand of music. He was undoubtedly the best at the short time he spent with us* (Smith 2017).

Mental illness is defined as a disease that causes mild to severe disturbances in thought and or behaviour, resulting in an inability to cope with life's ordinary demands and routines (Mental Health America 2018). It may cause changes in mood, personality, personal habits, and sometimes leads to withdrawal. It may be related to excessive stress due to a particular situation or series of events. It can be triggered by diverse factors including environmental or biological conditions, and as with other major diseases, has physical as well as emotional manifestations. There are over two hundred classified forms of mental illness (Mental Health America 2018), and at least one of these affected the venerable Don Drummond.

Drummond's mother took him to the Alpha Boy's School in East Kingston on December 9, 1943, at the tender age of 11. This was a school founded in the 1880s for wayward boys who would be educated and given practical training in a trade. She had become fed up with his bad behaviour, made worse by an absent father, and which included instances of truancy. It is not clear whether his mental illness was recognized then.

Alpha's musical programme grew, and by the 1940s and 1950s it was training the majority of Jamaica's leading musicians. David Katz reports that Rico Rodriguez, himself an internationally acclaimed and decorated trombonist, noted that: "Most that I know on trombone is what he [Don] taught me" (Katz 2013). At Alpha

Boys School, Rodriguez was a schoolmate and close friend of Drummond's and outlined what a typical day would entail at Alpha: "We don't go to school all day, like the average person. We go to school half-day, music half-day." Katz also documents the multitudinal challenges of that life, describing punishment for "wayward boys" as "brutal" – with "students routinely beaten or locked into understairs cupboards for perceived wrongdoings" (Katz 2013).

It was at Alpha that Drummond's talent blossomed. Under the guidance of bandmaster Tulloch, he quickly mastered the trombone which many of his peers found difficult. Another schoolmate who would also join him in the "Skatalites", Lester Sterling, was under no illusion as to his talent from the moment he enrolled in the school. "At Alpha, he was playing better than some of the guys who were playing two years before him." He took great pleasure entertaining fellow students as well as his teachers.

After spending seven years at the institution, Drummond decided that he had had enough and left. He was recommended to and accepted by the Eric Deans band where he became the main trombonist. At the time, the Eric Deans Orchestra was the leading ensemble band on the island. Although his stay was pretty short, he got the opportunity to broaden his horizons. This insight was provided by veteran entertainment journalist from the *Gleaner* and host of the popular programme, the "Saturday Night Alternatives" on *KLAS ESPN* sports radio, Roy Black: "A Caribbean tour by the band between 1951 and 1952 gave Drummond the opportunity to widen his musical horizons, gaining valuable experience in the process." Stints with Kenny Bradshaw's band and Kenny Williams' orchestra also proved beneficial to the teenager.

By the middle of the 1950s, Drummond, who by now was considered the island's top trombonist, became greatly influenced by current American blues which shaped his next set of recordings that included "Schooling the Duke", "Reload", and "Looking Through the Window". His stock continued to rise and he would eventually grab the attention of some of the luminaries in the industry at the time. Influential record producer Clement Dodd remarked, "It was a pleasure listening to Don solo. His execution was mild; he wasn't blaring; he was a very neat and first-class soloist."

Drummond eventually played with distinctive bands in the Kingston area, searching, it seems, until he became part of the "Skatalites" in 1963. Black believes that their similar backgrounds made it relatively straightforward for them to form the group, which consisted of Tommy McCook, Roland Alphonso, Lester Sterling (all saxophonists), Johnny Moore (aka Dizzy Johnny), Jackie Mittoo (pianist), Lloyd Knibb (drum), Lloyd Brevitt (bass player), and Jerry Haynes (guitarist). Despite disbanding shortly after they were formed, this combo played a pivotal role as they participated on several recordings by many Jamaican artistes in that era.

According to Clement Dodd, who went on to create the now famous Studio One, it was an undeniable fact that the band relied on Drummond's talent. Dodd was happy to be given the opportunity to work with Drummond when he was at the peak of his game:

> I was very happy working with him, because I knew of him before he started recording for me, but he went in the asylum; and when he came out, he came by me, because that time I was the leading sound system recording producer. He came to me because I was the new kid on the block, recording all the good artistes, and I didn't have any doubt. I [knew] he was a winner, so I signed him up on contract in 1961.

His illness was his biggest torment, and according to Dodd, this served as an unwanted interruption. "When I started recording he was there [in the studio] for about a year-and-a-half, and then he went back in the asylum. He was acting up, so his mother had to put him back in the asylum."

Julian "Jingles" Reynolds, who wrote the liner notes for the album *Don Drummond 100 Years After*, which contained the single "Don's Cosmic", says despite Drummond being a part of the "Skatalites" he was the main centre of attraction. Jingles recalls that:

> The music of the Skatalites was brilliant, but it was Don that most people wanted to hear and see. His musical genius and eccentricity had moved ahead of him, making fans in every nook and cranny where his music was played, fall in love with him. His easy but exquisitely professional command of his horn won him compliments from the great J.J. Johnson, the American jazz trombonist, composer and arranger. The exchanges between Drummond and Johnny Moore on trumpet were like a machine gun in full blast. His [trom]bone spoke sometimes like a trumpet high and cutting, and again it was like a baritone, heavy low and grumbling.

Vocalist, songwriter and producer Clancy Eccles in an interview with journalist Steve Barrow (cited in Katz 2013) highlighted examples of how fragile Drummond could get and how his frequent acts of tomfoolery seemed to defy all logic:

> While we were recording down by Federal, they was digging out that piece of land, and Don used to go over and pick up this pretty piece of clay and put it in his Ovaltine. Don Drummond never eat anything hot – everything cold, lot of fruits and so on. One day Roland [Alphonso] and Johnny [Moore] looked in the bottle, it was clay and all those things mixed together, and Drummond said, 'People are supposed to live in an atomic energy, you are supposed to build atoms inside of you' – that's why he ate the clay. For a madman, Drummond was extraordinary – I wouldn't call Drummond mad. There's another story of Don Drummond performing in Port Antonio, and the MC said, 'Now we present Don Drummond!' and Drummond just came right out, in a suit, and just pull down the zip and just piss on them! Drummond was just something else. Drummond never wear a shoe – always wear his felt hat, him look beautiful, but he's not wearing a shoe. He was like one of those American jazz musicians, just a different type of person.

Despite all of this, he continued to create waves, and as Black explains, Drummond and music were a perfect match:

> *Actually, Don Drummond, I think it was Alpha that influenced him to get into this trombone playing thing you know. Because, the general trend at Alpha at the time as I understand it, was for the music master or the school management to put you into some trade thing. I don't think that they usually ask you what you want to do.*
>
> *Don Drummond was placed in a band, in the Alpha Band. He was given a trombone. He was taught the instrument by the bandmasters, but he himself improvised. He was like a genius. He improvised all these stuff until he became almost like a competent trombonist by the time he left Alpha.*

His recordings seem to support this observation, as hits such as "Eastern Standard Time", "Music is my Occupation", "Addis Ababa", "Scrap Iron", "Far East", "Confucius", and "Man in the Street", "Dick Tracy", and "Green Island" figured prominently on the charts.

Black, who admired Drummond and has covered music for close to 40 years, says from the first time Don's music entered his consciousness, he was in no doubt he (Drummond) would have been great:

> I remember seeing him at a couple theatres in Kingston. I saw him at the Globe, and at Bournemouth Beach Club down by what they call Manley Boulevard now, or something like that. He was sort of an eccentric type of person. Because of the way he used to play the trombone, people used to just gravitate towards him. They just love how Don Drummond played that trombone, that's all. His music was just sweet. That's all I can tell you.

Both Black and Smith agreed that his mental illness and his unpredictability were part of the reason that he was so special. Black further recalls:

> Don Drummond was a strange guy, because sometimes you would go to see a performance, and the band start up and you don't see Don Drummond. He was not in there. People start wonder, 'What happen to this man? Where is Don Drummond? Where him is?' and all of a sudden you would start hear him blow from out the street. Is like him coming... him coming, but he hears the song from inside wherever it is being played, the club or wherever it is, or the theatre, and he just pick up his section, and just start blow and come in and join the band.
>
> I think it all had to do with his mental condition, because he was sort of having some mental things from he was very, very young. Him just by himself. Him hardly talk. His trombone was like his voice, because that's what he used to use to communicate with people.

Smith, who lived about two hundred yards from Drummond, says:

> Don did things all of us did but on several occasions he did some of the weirdest things you could ever imagine. He was the only musician that I ever saw who came to the bandstand with his instrument in the case all put together, sat down in front of everybody, open the case, take out the instrument, dissect it, pull the chamois from his pocket, shined the parts one by one, put them back together, got up and walked away without playing a note. Most of the times, it was my job to go bring him back. Some of the times, I wasn't able to. But there are the times when he would go through the same ritual and

when he got to the part where he would put his lips together and made that funny wiggle, you knew he was going to blow.

His dedication to the music, and eagerness to succeed often resulted in him being late for a set. According to Smith, he would practice for hours which would at times mean joining his band on stage midway into the performance. He would often be seen with sheets of music as well as many books detailing the successes of other world renowned trombonists such as J.J. Johnson, Kai Winding, Bennie Green and Curtis Fuller. Smith recollects:

Like the Sunday evening he was supposed to be on the bandstand at Bournemouth Club and Tommy McCook said to me, 'Go up into the hills and see if you can find him.' I took somebody's bicycle and rode all over Wareika Hill without any success. Decided to turn back and on my way down Seaview Avenue, I caught up to him walking with the case in his hand. He jumped on the bicycle and we got to the club. As I was about to go through the front he said, 'No man, I have something a want you fi hear before a go upstairs.' We went up the back stairs that led to the back of the stage. Without any ritual he started to play something I never heard before. Then he asked, 'You like it?'
I said, 'What is that?'
He said, 'You no like it?'
I said, 'I affi hear it again.'
He did it again and said, 'Weh you think?'
I said, 'I like it; but weh you get that from?'
He replied, 'Bwoy, that's what I was a work pon; that is why I late.'

His mental illness, according to many, perhaps played a significant role in the incident that brought his career to a screeching halt. This arguably will go down in Jamaica's history as being one of the most followed cases of murder, where jealousy, disobedience, love and disappointment were all mushroomed together. In his love for Anita "Margarita" Mahfood, a rhumba dancer and singer, Drummond was very obsessive and would react aggressively at the sight of another man dancing with his woman. Persistent warnings fell on deaf ears, and Margarita kept on doing what came naturally to her. As Smith picks up the story, he relates that he was one of the last persons to see her alive and berates himself for not doing things differently that fateful night:

It was about two o'clock in the morning. It was the ending of the Christmas holiday, New Year's night. A group of us had just ordered a drink in the Baby Grand [night club] in Cross Roads. Lenny Hibbert walks in, just finishing his gig at the VIP Lounge. We were just getting ready to kill the rest of the night when Margarita – Don's girlfriend – walks in [to the club] half dressed. She was still wearing whatever she was dancing in at the Cotton Club at Red Gal Ring, a popular entertainment spot in Kingston at the time. Margarita said, 'One a oono hafi carry me home. Junie [Don] a go kill mi wid beaten if him know seh me out yah.' He should have been playing at the Bournemouth Club with the Skatalites. Only he never showed up that night, and I wasn't there to go look for him. Well we were all good Samaritans, so Lenny suggested since I lived next door to him, I should follow him to Johnson Town where she lived. We took her home, watched her open the door and we drove off.

The next morning about 9:30, someone came up to me and said a news flash had just come on the Rediffusion that Donald killed Margarita last night. Of course you know that I refused to believe that, considering that I dropped her off not many hours ago. If she had been killed last night, we took home a ghost. Well yours truly waited for the next newscast and did not do any more work for the rest of the day.

She had been brutally murdered by Drummond who inflicted four stab wounds to her upper body. He was tried and found guilty of murdering his lover in 1965. Trial judge, the late Justice Fox (later Judge in the Court of Appeal) ordered that he be kept in strict custody as a criminal lunatic until the Governor General's pleasure was known (*Jamaica Observer* 2012a).

Former prime minister of Jamaica, the Most Hon. P.J. Patterson was one of the lawyers to represent Drummond in the trial. Patterson was acquainted with Drummond through the music as he at one point was manager for the "Skatalites" of which Drummond was a member (Patterson 2018). Patterson believes that Drummond was one of the finest trombonists Jamaica has ever seen.

On May 6, 1969 Drummond died at the Bellevue Hospital of natural causes.

His name and memory still evoke numerous debates among musicians as well as academics. His actions have become famous through the pens of poets who have written extensively on his career. These include Raymond Mair, Professor Mervyn Morris, Lorna Goodison, Robin "Jerry" Small, and Kwame Dawes. Goodison believes Drummond is popular with poets as his actions reflect the great tragic heroes of the past: "If you saw him on the stage, you did not look at anyone else... Some people just have that star quality." For Small, he brought out the smoothness in the music which not many could achieve: "Music is a thing that soothes and it also stirs. With Drummond, it was soothing." According to Herbie Miller (cited in Cooke 2016), the morning after killing Margarita, Don walked into the Rockfort Police Station and remarked, "A woman up the road killed herself with a knife." For Morris, Drummond's response to the police was very symbolic, but he insists that despite this, "I think it is the music that meant most to me."

On his music, Goodison was full of praise for the man who many described as a phenomenon: "It was like he had gathered some of our collective memories and was able to put it in his music. The atoms shift when you hear that music. There is not even any way you can explain anything like that."

In her email interview with David Katz early November 2013, Heather Augustyn, who published a book about the life of Don Drummond (2013), was in no doubt as to what drew her to write about him as a subject for a book:

> First, I fell in love with his music. I love the haunting wail of his trombone as its minor chords slide above the layered rhythms of Lloyd Knibb's drums, the upbeat mixed with the soulful. It is his compositions that made me first appreciate him as an artist. But then when I heard about his life, and I think I first heard about it actually from Lloyd Brevett in 1996, that's what piqued my interest as a writer. I wanted to know why, of course, like everyone does. I wanted to really find out what made him do such a terrible thing and what could drive a man with such immense talent and beauty to such horrors. It was a combination of admiration and curiosity (Katz 2013).

The rollercoaster nature of her research journey left an indelible mark on her life, and she concluded that despite the tragedy that surrounded Drummond, Jamaica has benefited from him a great deal. She also revealed some of her thinking which will astonish many:

I think the life of Margarita, Anita Mahfood, was the most surprising. No one ever talks about her. She was equally as amazing as Don. She was an artist in her own right with passion for life. So it was fascinating for me to uncover this woman, this spirit, and put together the details of her life to understand how she played such a vital role in the acceptance of Rastafarian music in the mainstream clubs. We really owe her a debt of gratitude for her tenacity and it makes me wonder where reggae music would be without her[1] (Katz 2013).

In an interview with the *Jamaica Observer*, Miller recalled how Margarita once stood up for the Count Ossie Troupe when show promoter Vere Johns refused to have a group of Rastafarians accompany her on stage for a performance at the Carib Theatre: "He didn't want them to go on because they were Rasta, and she said she would not do it (perform) unless they accompanied her, which was very principled" (Campbell 2013).

Also surprising was discovering the types of treatment that Don received, or was subjected to, at Bellevue, and not surprising was that death resulted from such barbaric treatment.[2]

Controversially, asked whether or not Drummond could have achieved more if it were not for restrictions placed on him by producers who purely wanted to stick to a ska beat, she was rather philosophical:

---

1   Margarita's contributions were acknowledged in a ceremony hosted by the University of Technology (UTECH) on April 11, 2013 where she was recognized along with a group of women for years of service to the music industry. Despite her only having recorded one track ("Woman a Come") for producer Arthur Duke Reid, Herbie Miller who had recommended her, believed she was an unsung hero of early Jamaican music, especially as she defended Rastafarians at a time when discrimination and persecution against them were at their highest point.

2   Such treatment included "patients given drugs to sedate them and electro shock therapy". This was confirmed by other musicians as well as relatives of the Senior Medical Officer (SMO) who was present at the time. The SMO's daughter remarked: "EST was definitely the thing, electroshock. The medication would have been basically heavy sedatives. There were basically things to kind of conk you out. Drummond was pretty zonked out from early on." See haugustyn, "Bellevue Mental Hospital"– blog post (October 2013). http://old.skabook.com/foundationska/2013/10/bellevue-mental-hospital/

I wouldn't say it was hindered by ska, but I do see that point of view because for Don Drummond, music was his occupation. He played what he was told. In the clubs he played the jazz standards for the tourists. In the studio he played what would sell. When Coxsone [Clement Seymour "Sir Coxsone" Dodd, Jamaican record producer] said write the 'Trolley Song' from [the film] *Meet Me in St. Louis*, he did 'Further East'. That's what hindered him, the business of ska, and the business of jazz. Creatively he was limited by what would sell. I'm sure many musicians can identify with that. Had he not had to sing for his supper he could have branched out to do who knows what. And he could have ventured into other genres too, especially as they were coming along. Can you imagine what he would have had to say with his horn during the soul years, the funk years, and the avant-garde jazz years? (see Katz 2013).

She revealed that it made her sick that despite his genius he was not able to fully overcome his challenges:

We hear stories of triumph all of the time – Oprah is full of them, she herself is one of them; and Elvis and Johnny Cash and Loretta Lynn and the list goes on and on. I teach my own boys that if you work hard and never give up and you develop your skill and your passion, you can be a success or be fulfilled with your life. That's what we all learn, right? But it kills me to know that is not true. Here is an example of someone who despite immense talent and drive and hard work was not able to overcome the challenges of poverty and mental illness and struggle (cited in Katz 2013).

For Black, Drummond's biggest legacy is the music that he did and left with us. He believes his influence stretches far and wide and many of today's trombonists and horn players have been influenced by his works. Drummond's memories, according to him, will live on for generations to come and his exploits will never be surpassed:

He will be remembered, as far as I know, as Jamaica's greatest trombonist, and one of the persons that laid the foundation of Jamaica's early ska music. Because, as you know, ska was the foundation of Jamaican music. Even the foundation of what they now call 'dancehall'. It all started with ska. Don Drummond was there from the beginning, and he was one of the main contributors to that development in the early days. Because, believe it or not, although Tommy McCook and Roland Alphonso were popular and Tommy McCook was the leader, Don Drummond was really the star of the band.

Whatever is said, Don Drummond will go down in history as one of the best trombonists to have ever lived. What makes it all the more remarkable is that he died at 37, an age when most musicians are about to enter their prime years. He became popular across spheres of influence and broke down barriers that were socially erected by society about persons with disabilities. One can only conceive what would have happened to Drummond in a modern context where there are greater support services for persons with mental disabilities. Medical treatment has advanced significantly and once the person with mental illness is taking the prescribed medication, there will be mental stability. Furthermore, once there is strong family support and understanding in the community, the person with the mental illness is likely to function normally. Environmental factors contribute immensely to mental illness and one can only speculate on what transpired in his early life when he developed the mental problem.

Those of us who assess the cultural contribution of persons with disabilities would have liked for this iconic trombonist to have experienced modern medical treatment and care. Undoubtedly, he would be a mega-star. Some 50 years after his death, the world is still craving for his music. Such is the potency and magnetism of Drummond's music through which he made a significant contribution to Jamaica's culture. This is a way that one can measure the magnitude of the contribution of an individual to a particular sector or development.

Don Drummond – musician extraordinaire with mental disability.

Askhelle: The King of Beats

Life hard but don't give up,
  me suffer like dog but me hold it out
Regular me trod down the hungry road,
  prosperity after the drought
Ghetto youth hold the faith and pray;
  Jaja naa gi yu more dan yu can bear
Me afi tell di ghetto yutes dem ole on,
  when me remember we me a come from
One pants, one shoes, one dutty lean Clarkes,
  one pants, one dutty lean Clarkes
Hold di faith and pray, don't stop;
  rain no fall pan one man ouse tap.

(Vybz Kartel produced by Askhelle 2011)

In this chapter, we turn to one of the modern "dynamos" of music in Jamaica. This visually impaired but exquisitely talented man has been contributing to the transformational beats in the music industry in Jamaica since the mid-2000s. This case study has brought to light rich details of the life of one of the hidden treasures in Jamaican music – Michael Fairman.

The name Michael Fairman or "Askhelle" as he is commonly known, does not readily resonate with those who are not intimately connected with the music industry. In other words, one would not say that Michael Fairman is a household name that rolls easily off the average tongue. However, this talented young specialist has slowly but steadily eked out a niche for himself in this rather competitive and growing business. A former student of the Salvation Army School for the Blind and Visually Impaired, situated at 57 Mannings Hill Road in Kingston, Fairman envisioned involving himself deep in the field of music. According to him, "When I was four, I vision that I was doing a song titled, 'What We Need in This World'. However, I did not do the song until nine years later."

Introduction into the Business

Fairman's early introduction to the music started back in 1994 when he recalls arriving at school. "Some boys were having a conversation centred on a keyboard. At the time, I did not even know what a keyboard was but I asked my mother to buy it." His acquisition of this equipment placed Fairman's feet firmly on the musical path. While the average 10-year-old boy was fascinated with football, cricket and other commonplace social activities, at that age Fairman was profoundly concentrated on how to launch his musical career.

His "game" was music. Forget the ordinary sports of athletics and volleyball; those were for lesser mortals. Askhelle had his head so firmly pointed in the direction of becoming one of Jamaica's superstars in the industry that he acquired a manager – one of his boyhood friends, the late I-Roy Johnson, who also loved and appreciated the industry. His early love for the music led him to form a mouth organ group with his peers at age 12. Drawing an analogy from the Bible, like Jesus at age 12, he saw himself as being "about his father's business". At this rather young age, his voracious appetite for the music had him avidly listening to composers like Steelie and Clevie, Sly and Robbie, Computer Paul, and Donny Browning.

Askhelle shared: "When it comes onto R&B, I listened to Baby Face, R. Kelly, and Rodney Jerkins." He continued:

I did not choose music – music chose me. There were times when I tried to avoid the keyboard, but I was drawn back to it through some unknown force. Over the years, the industry has taught me certain things. For example, I am a very outspoken person, but I have realized that you can't say everything. Certain things have to be swept under the carpet. The industry has honed my ability to be patient and calm.

Since the inception of his professional career, he has learned more and more from the field. He notes that one of his biggest challenges in the industry as a visually impaired person is being paid – particularly by his fellow Jamaicans. "Foreigners pay me more quickly than some of my fellow Jamaicans."

Fairman built a huge reputation for himself as a singer, songwriter, producer and creator of beats, because of the high standards he set in the industry. Accomplished individuals in the field such as Sean Nizzle unhesitatingly recommended Askhelle at every opportunity: "Yu know I have a brethren who bad pan di keyboard! . . ."

One of his biggest accomplishments thus far is to have been the composer of a plethora of number one hit songs on the local and international scene. These include "Turn and Wine" and "Bad Reputation" (Vybz Kartel); "Pan de Ting" and "Always on My Mind" (Mavado); "Night and Even Day", "Life", and "Just a Little Bit Longer" (G Whiz); "If You Blame Life" (Bugle); "Real Friends" (Chris Martin, D Major, and Agent Sasco); and "Candle in the Wind" (Tahz). All of these came about due to his productive brilliance and wizardry at creating musical beats.

Fairman commands great respect and admiration from several artistes. He is highly sought after by many who hold him in high esteem. However, he lamented:

> Everybody who comes to me tend to think that I can give them a hit record. I am clueless as to why this perception is out there. People in the business think that I am more talented than my sighted counterparts; however, this does not always translate into their willingness to pay more quickly.

According to Askhelle, the industry does have its challenges. In an interview, he told Shavane Daley – one of the researchers on this project – that he had even received death threats as a result of refusing to play for certain persons. "When you are good, you are up against a lot of things – for instance, bad-mouthing."

However, this does not deter Fairman from continuing to deliver quality products. Although he does not let down his guard in a volatile society, he remains positive that he has sufficiently covered his back to ward off undesirables, many of whom now enter the industry as the advent of the computer has made this easier. "With more computers, those who cannot afford high-end equipment can always enter as it is less expensive. However, I have not abandoned my drum machines and keyboard. The conflation of the computer and the manual equipment serves to heighten the quality of the production."

He acknowledges that while working with the popular producer Arthur Wale, he got very little recognition or financial reward. However, in our interview, he noted that the experience gained was phenomenal. When asked about the direction he would like the industry to take, Askhelle responded by saying, "I would like more conscious music on the radio. A lot of garbage is being played these days."

Fairman bemoans the improper crediting of work, a feature that is very much a part of the profession which is having a poisonous effect. It occurs where an individual who contributes to the production of a particular record is not given proper recognition for his or her time and effort, and all credit goes to the producer. He insists that this must be eradicated from the industry; failing which, the music will suffer. "This factor has cost me dearly; I would love to see it removed from the industry."

For a visually impaired person coming into music, Fairman argues that it demands a significant amount of patience and dedication. The industry is dominated by the sighted, and for someone with a visual disability to succeed, he or she has to work doubly hard as it takes more time to master the craft. At present, his label, Vision House, promises great things. "There is great promise! There is great talent emerging like myself. I am working on my first One-drop album at present. Do expect international artistes on the label soon. There is a young lady from Barbados; she is really good. There is also Barbie (not the popular one) from the United States who is slated to make an appearance on the label," he proudly explains.

He cherishes tremendous dreams for himself within the music. In fact, he is quite excited about its future. "I would like to collaborate with Rodney Jerkins, R. Kelly, and Stephen Marley." Certainly, he aims at reaching for the stars while he remains in the business.

Musical Partner

Damion "DJ Cane" Rose has known Fairman for most of his life. From their early years at the Salvation Army School for the Blind and Visually Impaired, Rose detected Fairman's inborn love for music. It was deeply buttressed in his soul. "He was into R&B pop music. We talked about music a lot; I could see his deep love for music even then."

Fairman and Rose have worked closely together for several years. In 2007 they formed the music label, Vision House, which has aided the emergence of several new artistes, many of whom have produced chart busters. In their early days at school, the two were a part of a singing group "TOF" which staged many concerts all over the island. Rose recalls that the grounds of the French embassy was one of the many venues at which the group performed. "Our working relationship spans 14 years so far," he notes.

According to Rose, Fairman did not only produce, but he sang as well, which even preceded his work as a producer. "He does a healthy imitation of the Jamaican artiste Buccaneer, and the international artiste R. Kelly." He confirmed that Fairman does have an album in the pipeline, but lamented the fact – also noted by Fairman – that one of his greatest challenges was receiving payment after doing work for artistes. This phenomenon seemed to have strong links to his visual disability which appeared to be the basis of the refusal of unscrupulous individuals to pay, even as they lauded the quality of his work. "We are always willing and able to help out other artistes or experts in the field, but these persons are most times hesitant to pay their way... People don't seem to think that we need money like anybody else." Rose argued that the fact that both he and Fairman were visually impaired as producers meant that their colleagues took them for granted when money was the issue.

However, he observed that Fairman's impact was tremendous, as others endeavoured to pattern him in their own music production. "His inclination to willingly share his vast understanding of the music has significantly assisted me. He is not mean and clumsy with his knowledge, and this is partly responsible for my growth in the profession." Based on their working relationship, he foresees great things in the proverbial pipeline. "We plan to return the music to the good days, not necessarily playing back the type of music that existed then, but we intend to put back the good quality into the music that was once there."

Fairman's record label continues to attract several quality artistes. This is largely attributed to the high quality of the work that he delivers and to the appreciation expressed by his satisfied clients. He has worked with iconic figures like Sly and Robbie, Danny Brownie, Gussy Clarke, and Sean Nizzle in the past. For blind and visually impaired artistes, Rose argues, "If you are talented and knowledgeable, the music industry can be rewarding for persons with disabilities. I encourage any person with a disability to get his house in order if he intends to become a part of the profession." But he opines that though there are rewards to be gained, the music industry also has its drawbacks, even for talented persons like Fairman. "It is a 'dog eat dog' industry. One can be easily exploited if he does not have his wits about him. On the other hand, though it is hard and grinding work, if the blind and visually impaired person is committed and willing to put in the hard work, success can be reaped."

Rose envisions even greater success for Fairman if he continues to work hard and does not comprom

on quality. A person with a disability must understand that because of the competitive nature of the music and entertainment industry, he or she must engage in high quality work in order to reap success. Exceptional quality must become a way of life for the people with a disability, in whatsoever area of life they choose.

Hidden Treasure

Ricardo McCarthy, "Wowski", has been working with Fairman for over a year. Together they have completed a 15-track album. Tracks like "99 Storm" and "Colour the World Like a Crayon" have done quite well on both the local and international circuits. Fairman's reputation as a quality producer is paying off for him.

Wowski, a songwriter, learned of Fairman through dancehall artist QQ's manager, who thought that his lyrics were best suited for Fairman's type of production. It was through their first encounter that he discovered that Fairman was visually challenged: "I was handing this brother the CD and he was not responding to me. I began to wonder what was wrong with him." On discovery of the impairment he became even more impressed with Fairman's many accomplishments, and after he produced his first song, his amazement leapt. He was further intrigued by Fairman's exceptionally high standards:

> I choose to work with Askhelle because he is a brilliant producer. If this man can produce such fine rhythms without full sight, his hearing must be greater than that of the sighted producer. His ability to meet international standards at such an alarming rate is nothing short of marvellous. His high energy is contagious; furthermore, I like his commitment to detail. Fairman's loyalty and honesty as a producer speak volumes for him.

Wowski hopes that Askhelle's career would get the proverbial shot in the arm because of his reputation for the highest standards and his adherence to the highest quality. When quizzed about Fairman's major achievements thus far, he spelt it out:

He has built nuff riddims. Some have managed to reach the Bill-board – for example, Mavado's 'Unchanging Love' produced by DJ Khaled from the United States. Most of the music wi hear pan di radio, im have a han in it. His involvement in the lives of many youth who could have turned to a life of crime is significant. He has given me a sense of hope, a sense of direction that I can now fulfil my purpose on earth through di production of my music globally.

His reputation for professionalism and his character, along with his immense knowledge, are the bases on which he predicts that Fairman's contribution to the industry will reap him great reward someday. Wowski's view is that he will get due recognition at some point in his career as he is a unique individual in spite of the impediment that encumbers him.

And his ultimate endorsement: "Askhelle is one of Jamaica's hidden treasures; one of the island's best-kept secrets that must someday be unveiled for all to see. If it is incumbent upon me to promote this producer for him to get his due deserts, I will."

Dancehall's Best Kept Secret

Another artiste who has harvested tremendous success as a result of his activity with Askhelle is reggae singer Tahz. He has been working with him for eight years and describes him as one of the finest musicians with whom he has ever worked: "I have been working with Askhelle from 2009... I met him through one of my friends, Ricky G., who described him as a musical genius." He says his first impression of Fairman confirmed that description. "It was miraculous. He was in fact a genius! I was stunned by his ability. Knowing that he was visually impaired and could do what he did, I was stunned! His beats are current and him ting up to date."

Tahz credits Askhelle with playing a major role as manager in his biggest single to date, which has topped many charts in Europe as well as in Jamaica, the homeland of reggae: "Askhelle is a great beat composer. He is also a great singer and songwriter. He is responsible for giving me my number one song 'Candle in the Wind'." They have also collaborated on other songs such as "Body Language", "Parables of the Street", "One Pants", and "God Bless Ma Soul".

In Tahz's opinion, Askhelle's musical talent and his attitude as a leader in the industry make him stand out. He describes him as a perfectionist, unique, and as one who is trying to be himself and no one else. One of the things he respects about him is his vision for the music: "Him pre the music pan a deeper level dan most other producer." He perceives Fairman's input, his contribution to the culture of Jamaica, as major:

> Whether it may be Kartel or Mavado, him mek beat for dem man de song. Him have a lot of hits out there. Him mek riddim for nuff a di producer or work with nuff of the composer in dancehall and reggae like TJ, Tryton, Sean Nizzle, Birch, Sukko, and many many more. Me always tell him dat him is one of the best kept secrets in the dancehall. He has created so many hit rhythms but lacks the requisite recognition for them. What I want to see is Askhelle being given the honour he deserves, so that the world can know who is behind all these producers and artistes for them to get these hits songs. Song like 'Take It' by Mavado and [singer like] Karian Sang, which also made the Billboard.

Riddims (beats) composed by Askhelle for various producers and artistes include: "Compassion", "Contagious", "Word of Prayer", "DNA", "Alter Ego", "Mood Swing", "Energize", "Dutty Sneakers", "You Gone", "True Emotions" (featuring Shawn Nizzle), "One Chance" (featuring Birch), and "Sweet Dreams".

Michael "Askhelle" Fairman is another of Jamaica's many hidden diamonds, quietly helping to build on the country's rich musical heritage. Though he does this with hardly any recognition, he does not fuss about his obscurity. Instead, he soldiers on and uplifts the lives of myriad youths who are struggling to survive. The many testimonies to this man's worth show the quality that can emanate from individuals in spite of their circumstances. Blindness or limited vision has only served to sharpen his resolve and make him more committed to the task at hand. Fairman will continue to shine and leave his mark indelibly inscribed on the proverbial sands of time.

In the meantime, people continue to sing and dance to the pulsating rhythms created by a man who is visually impaired, without care or clue as to the circumstances of the talent behind the music. But it continues to make an impact as they enjoy themselves at clubs, parties, dances or wherever they meet to socialize. It is, however, heartening to know that a visually impaired man is making such a major contribution to the cultural advancement of Jamaica.

Israel Vibration: The Trio
That Nearly Never Made It

There is no end, to a good thing, oh no
'Cause every day there is Jah loving, yeah
Principalities and powers
Them planning war on the hour, yes
A spiritual wickedness in a high places

I saw the children cry;
I saw the children die;
I saw much fuss and fights
Against the truths and rights
Jah love within, stronger than their sins
Them just can't conquer Jah love within, oh no

Keep it up Jah children
Livin' up your roots, well, well
Every tree stays up by its roots, yeah
A make we sing and shout, tell it all about
Jah Jah live and reign, and He is still the same.

(Israel Vibration 1997)

Formed in 1973 Israel Vibration, a roots-reggae band, has become one of the most powerful and captivating musical trios to emerge from Jamaica. The unique group comprised Lascelle "Wiss" Bulgin, Albert "Apple Gabriel" Craig, and Cecil "Skeleton (Skelly)" Spence, who were all stricken with polio in their youth and were patients at the Sir John Golding Rehabilitation Centre where they met. These were particularly trying times for Jamaica in the mid to late 1950s, as the country was undergoing a polio epidemic which claimed the lives of many and disabled many others.

Poliomyelitis, or polio, is a highly contagious disease caused by a virus that attacks the nervous system. Children younger than five years old are more likely to contract the virus than any other group. It enters the body through the intestines where it spreads into the bloodstream and destroys the nervous system and motor neurons which control muscle movements. One per cent of victims are paralyzed. It is significant that all the members of Israel Vibration fell into this cohort.

As was customary for children with disabilities who came from poor backgrounds, all three were sent to the Centre in Kingston as their parents were unable to care for them. However, despite being surrounded by other students with similar conditions, they never adapted entirely to their new situation and surroundings at the Rehabilitation Centre.

Their disabilities, coupled with their chronic financial positions, all contributed to making the environment challenging, as it was insensitive to their needs. To overcome such circumstances, one has to dig deep into one's inner reserves to find the formula for success. This is what led to the trio drawing on their musical talents, having attempted other pursuits in the effort to make ends meet.

Bulgin had spent the majority of his early years at different rehabilitation centres and had even worked for a tailor in his teens. Spence was also a member of the National Wheelchair Basketball team. His fortunes took a turn for the worse in 1969, when he was dropped from the team because of his conversion to Rastafarianism. At that time, the Rastafarian lifestyle was ridiculed, and members often faced discrimination and physical abuse from the authorities and the general society.

Craig was the closest to music as he attended the renowned Alpha Boys School (also known as the Alpha Cottage School) for a brief period. This technical and vocational institution had a rich history in music. Some of the individuals who passed through its doors included members of the Skatalites, and drummer Leroy "Horse Mouth" Wallace. Craig found the rigid structure hard to manage and ran away to a life of homelessness and poverty at age 14.

Of the three, Spence was the most talented and played xylophone for a youth band. He had gone back to the country after he had been dropped from the basketball team, but returned to Kingston after a couple of years. On his return, he bumped into Craig when travelling around town, and both met up with Bulgin. Their bond became even closer, as all three had by now converted to Rastafarianism. They decided to embrace music as their vocation, as their way out of poverty, and began singing at various events. As the saying goes, the rest is history.

In an interview with the *Riverfront Times* in 1996, Apple Gabriel outlined the early years of the group, starting with their debut in 1974. He recalled that their first performance was at the Theological College on Golding Avenue, right next door to the Rehabilitation Centre. He explained:

> *It was just the three of us and me playing the piano. Soon we hook up with a bredrin named Hugh Booth from the Twelve Tribes of Israel and he put out our first single. 'Why Worry' was a big hit and that success link us up with [producer] Tommy Cowan. We then do the* **Same Song** *album in '75 and it was released in '76. After that, we put out two 45s from it: 'Lift Up Your Conscience' and the title track. We then did a disco 45 named 'Crisis' and the last 45 we did was 'Never Gonna Hurt Me Again'. That was 1980, and was our last song using Tommy Cowan [as manager].*

The hits kept on coming, however, and that led them to the attention of Bob Marley whose Tuff Gong studio was the next port of call. According to Apple Gabriel, this was a breathtaking experience:

> *It's one of them groups that has an extremely unique sound; you can't miss Israel when you hear them. As you hear them you know is Israel. Especially in them whole harmony structure, the backup people what they do... their harmony is not fancy harmony; it's pretty basic. There is a style. You know how Eddy Fitzroy had a style about him? You know when he sang, you know it's Eddy Fitzroy... a strange sort of vibrato in the vocals. In music we call it vibrato.*

Tommy Cowan, musician, singer-songwriter and record producer, and one-time manager and producer of Israel Vibration was awarded a national honour – the Order of Distinction, Commander Class (CD). He is in no doubt that the shared determination between them, the collective message resonating from within and the will to overcome their adversities made them unique. He says:

> *The fact was that they were victims of polio disease and were determined to make it big and ultimately follow their dreams. At the same time, you had Bunny Wailer, Peter Tosh, and Bob Marley and the Wailers, and for some reason it was always on my mind that,*

Wow! These guys were almost like the Wailers in a different physical form! That for me was really special.

Cowan, who worked on two albums with the trio, was also instrumental on tracks such as "Friday Evening", "Mr Taxman", "Licks and Kicks and Box", "Give I Grace", "Walk the Streets of Glory", and "Weep and Moan".

Their discipline when it came to making music was, according to him, "different from what the normal person would think as discipline". It was so meticulous, even he as their producer disliked it at times. "They meshed together on certain disciplines for what they were about at that time and what they were to attain out of the business. They believed in themselves and so we had gone through a period at that time where there were a lot of suspicions surrounding them [because of their disability and Rastafarianism], and so they defended each other when it came to their music."

Cowan says that when they turned up at the studio to rehearse, they would do ten songs and an album, and each person in the group had to do three songs individually, which could take several hours. They were the quintessence of organization and discipline. "They never came into the studio and tried to sort out what they were about. They knew exactly what they wanted and rehearsed before coming in there."

Intense internal competition ensured that they got the best out of each other, but this, according to Cowan, led to serious differences and animosity between them from time to time:

I think they had a certain amount of difference sometimes when it came to each other on a personal level. Sometimes you felt there was a degree of jealousy in certain things. For instance, when they had to sing and then we had to choose the song. [They would] ask the producer to decide what [was to be sung] on stage and if one person had to sing many songs, there was a feeling of jealousy there.

Misconceptions by many artistes in that era made Cowan's job more difficult as he not only had to be battling internal rivalries between members but also outside influences. Some artistes felt that producers were cheating them and that they were not getting proper reward for their work. Members of Israel Vibration had this uncanny feeling as well. According to Cowan:

During that period of time, there was a feeling amongst several artistes that they were being cheated by producers. There were suspicions that records were being sold and they, the artistes, weren't seeing the returns. There was also this feeling that there was so much money in the business, and they thought we, the producers, ought to have been taking care of their everyday needs.

For example, if I [the artiste] have a car and if I have a child and he/she is sick, you [the producer] must take care of the child. You become the mother, the father and everything. Those were some of the demands that you found. As a matter of fact, I remember there was a time that I put some money together and said to the guys that they had to find a place to live, and we actually found the place where they should go and live. I'm not even sure how they were living at the time but it wasn't under good circumstances.

Craig was living across the gully down in the river bank. One day I went down there and he had some problems with some people there and they were trying to throw stones at him, I guess because of his behaviour towards his neighbours or whatever; and I said no, these guys got to get out of here. Because if he stayed there, people were going to hurt him. So I got this money together; but instead of them using the money to get the place, they shared up the money and one of them bought a car, and the next thing I know I see him coming say the car run out of gas.

I even remember times I would go out and I'm coming home at twelve, one o'clock in the morning, and they're laying down by my door step and saying that they want money. And I even remember one time I saw my flower pots mashed up because they said they were waiting on me and I didn't come home.

Despite all of this, Cowan never walked out on them, to the amazement of other producers and engineers. He even quipped that once, Errol Brown, one of the engineers, remarked how much he would regret his decision to stick around. He (Brown) even compared the group to Cowan's hands and feet – permanent fixtures on his body. Ironically, he felt working alongside them taught him above everything, how to be tolerant. "Sometimes in life when things come on me that are negative I can always say I've been there already and I picked the positive out of it."

But these guys were also very unpredictable. One day they would be very nice and another time they would be miserable. And how was Cowan able to deal with their unpredictability? "As a producer, you always have to be very diplomatic, in a sense. I'm not sure about every other producer but for me I never liked confrontation. I never liked fuss and fight so I always try to find a way to keep the calm."

In 1981 they migrated to the United States, but the first few years were difficult. According to Apple Gabriel:

God knows what would have happened if [we] were to just stick to Jamaica. I don't know that it would have worked... because Jamaica is very unforgiving. They don't really care who you are. If you are not putting up any fancy money to get airplay and you are not a social climber to engage yourself with people in terms of 'push up' to people and 'suck up' to people to get work, you know, [we] wouldn't be that type so [we] would have a difficulty here.

Cowan initially was apprehensive and concerned as to how they would manage in a foreign land. But after doing a deal for their product distribution with RAS Records, one of the major reggae music distribution networks in the world at the time, Cowan confessed that that was when he began to rest easy as he knew they were in good hands.

The collective decision was then taken for them to split up in order to make income flow easier for them and guarantee their survival. In this period, they produced and released "Cool and Calm", "Jah Love Me", "Payday," "Greedy Dog", "Don't Want Apartheid", "Perfect Love", "Understanding", "Live and Give", "Middle East", and "Strength of My Life".

According to Cowan:

Being victims of polio, you know they are not quite like regular people. But what they have achieved is remarkable because, you see, the music business is very rough and it's just a handful of people with disabilities that really don't fall through the cracks. It has been remarkable that they have sustained their sound, held together and have done well. They have had good management. There's a gentleman from France that is their manager, booking agent and thing, and so they were fortunate in that sense to get there on the world stage.

But Cowan thinks that more could have been achieved if they had remained together:

Let me say this. I'm proud that they are still there as a touring group but I'm disappointed that the three of them are not together; because Israel Vibration is really now Wiss and Skelly. It is just two of them, and I think Roots Radics is the band that backs them and so they are still touring. I am happy about that, but disappointed because I think that the three of them together would make a bigger impact.

I understand that they do not get along as a group. I don't know what the deep problem is between them, but as a group, if they had stuck together, I believe that they could have been very close to building something like the Wailers.

His Imperial Majesty Emperor Haile Selassie I of Ethiopia along with Jah and the Rasta culture's elder named Baba Douse had significant impact on their religious outlook. These teachings came in handy when they were constantly bombarded with questions and harassment from people about their condition. In the aforementioned interview with the *Riverfront Times*, Apple Gabriel was quite candid about his feelings about polio and the lasting effects it has had on his life: "It take a lot from me outta life, but at the same time it give me much more in life."

In an interview with Grub Cooper about the group, Apple Gabriel posited:

If you make music a career, then obviously you have to be prepared to take the ups and downs. It's like a man who opens a business, you can't be successful from the get-go. You will have robbery, fires, you get wiped out by various things, market forces, but you have to rise above all of that until you reap success. There's nothing in life that doesn't have ups and downs and like I've said, they've dealt with it very, very well. The road wouldn't be easy for them having the disabilities, but they obviously are very strong-minded and very determined so other musicians can take that kinda thing from them. They can emulate the determination and the commitment to what they believe in. They have impacted it [Jamaica's culture], but not in a direct way, because they would fall into the bracket of a roots group, just like maybe the Abyssinians – people like that who are heavily into black, into African, into Rastafari. So they are there but I couldn't honestly say the influence is great because you have not had a group that has tried to emulate that kind of style like they did.

Cowan took a different view and argued that they will be remembered as unsung heroes:

I believe that one day somebody will take up their catalogue and they will look at the words and the lyrics that they have written and the uniqueness of it in the time, and how relevant it was, and maybe wonder why people didn't pay more attention. Of course, there are people who pay attention to them, that's why they are still touring today. You have people who have paid attention to them and have found their music to be inspiring. People classify them as roots, as message, as consciousness; but people have not brought that consciousness to the top of the table to say, 'Here is a group that is alongside the Burning Spear; here is a group that is alongside the Wailers; the Marleys; Tosh. And that is where they are supposed to be placed.

He further opined that regardless of what there was in a person's life, the fact that one had vision was the most powerful thing: "Self-discipline is the highest form of living, and the eyes that look are common but eyes that see are rare."

History can be very unkind to some people, but one thing for sure is that Israel Vibration has played its part in the advancement of reggae music. They have overcome great adversities and have triumphed against the odds. Whether one considers their physical impairment or their financial stresses, through their musical talents they overcame it all. They never gave up, despite their physical disability or the disabling conditions they experienced in the Jamaican society. Not even when they felt that they were being cheated by producers, did they flicker. Despite the expectations of many members of the community of persons with disabilities in Jamaica, the members of Israel Vibration did not use their disability as a means of leveraging welfare support from the society. Instead, they held their heads high, focused on the prize and kept on pressing forward. Theirs was a constant search for better and for excellence.

Their story reminds one of the game of dominoes where, though a player may draw a bad hand, winning is still a possibility and is heavily dependent on how you play! They played their drawn hands with dignity. They might not have won everything. However, as persons with disabilities, they stamped their mark indelibly on Jamaica's culture through their music.

Damion "DJ Cane" Rose

Another person who is blind who is making his contribution to the music industry is Damion Rose. Damion enters the arena through sound system operating and is renowned for being an exciting and entertaining music master.

Known professionally as "DJ Cane", he is a disc jockey and an audio engineer living and operating in Kingston, Jamaica. Though totally blind, he fell in love with music production from a tender age and today works with a lot of veteran artistes and producers within the local music industry. Many have frowned upon persons with physical challenges who have developed a passion for music and who operate in this area. But despite the myriad trials, this is a field in which many people who are blind and or otherwise disabled have excelled. DJ Cane explains how his musical odyssey was inspired:

> I can remember my grandfather sitting down humming to the gospel tunes that were being played in the house. Then after the gospel they would play the country and westerns, and then in the evening you would hear your Percy Sledge and Billy King. This was the mid-80s for me. So I started loving the music from back then, and as friends use to say at the Salvation Army School for the Blind, anywhere you see a radio you will see me. Once there is something playing from a speaker, I would be there. So I had the influence coming from home, then at the School for the Blind.

In addition, DJ Cane notes that his major influence came from a sound system called "Small Axe" that played next door to the School for the Blind compound:

> Small Axe for me was my university where music was concerned. And I guess Small Axe [drove] the way in which I now play music – in that they played chronologically. So if they playing disco, this

week, they would play disco from the 1970s and then next week, they will play disco from the 1980s; same thing for the souls; same thing for the rock steady. So they gave you all genres of music. It helped me when I started to play.

While at the Salvation Army School for the Blind and Visually Impaired, DJ Cane and his friends would often discuss their love for music and their hope to one day become selectors in the industry. Some youngsters at the school saw this as the best means of making it in life. Despite the fact that his peers were more interested in becoming street DJs, he was at the time focused on radio. He says he was primarily inspired by certain radio presenters:

I remember while I was at school, couple guys and myself always wanted to do selecting. I guess this was also driven by Small Axe because we always listened to them, and radio was another driving force. I was always wanting to play music and talk. I always admired the folks who did it, so I would always listen to a lot of [radio presenters] Winston Williams, Tony Young and Alan Magnus.

Realizing the Dream

DJ Cane recalls that between 2009 and 2010, the availability of computers became widespread throughout the Jamaican society. More and more persons started making use of this technology. So he started researching software that he could use to enhance the playing of music from his laptop. He says:

I wanted to know how I could get software to play music because I wanted to play music. So starting out first for me, I used to use VLC and Windows Media Player. Believe it or not, those were my first set of mixing tools. After mastering this craft I started to show other persons. It was kinda hard for them, because you don't really have a monitor head; you had to just choose the songs and you listen through an output speaker. The only thing you had in your ears was JAWS telling you what the name of the song is, and in order for you to choose you had to move the headphone slightly and listen to what is going on on the outside speaker and try and play the tune. So that's how I mastered that.

JAWS is the acronym for Job Access With Speech. It is software that converts text to speech so that a person who is blind can independently navigate the computer. With this great invention, DJ

Cane became a true brand ambassador for the music. He was now in a position where people were beginning to see his talent. He disclosed how it all transpired:

> My first real play-out came at a bar. A friend of mine named Peter Chin had a bar on Mannings Hill Road and my friend Orell ('DJ Velvet') and I, we started playing there. Peter said we know music and the bar needs to have some music, you know; music makes your bar lively. So that's how we started. We started playing music, people [started] seeing us, yeah. We got a lot of liquor out of that.

Both DJ Cane and DJ Velvet were grateful for the exposure. They were not paid; but acquiring popularity was most important to them at that juncture of their careers. They were able to augment the numbers in the bar, and as a consequence the bar attracted more business. Invariably, the DJs benefited significantly from the added publicity, and more doors of opportunity continued to swing open for them.

DJ Cane shared an experience about a client who literally turned up at their door one day:

> We met a man called Bryan who owned a club called Flavaz also on Mannings Hill Road. The first time he came he was very impressed. I wasn't there. Orell was playing and when I came and started playing he was even more impressed and he said, 'Look here, I want to start an Oldies Sunday and I want you guys to play.'

This opportunity was marked by a misfortune that quickly evolved into an even greater good. DJ Cane gave a detailed breakdown of their play-out at the first Oldies Sunday:

> We went and we string up and we decided that we were gonna play in half-hour or one-hour sets, depending on how smoothly the music was flowing. So I told Orell to go first, so he started playing. Now when it was time for me to play, I took the headphones but I could not hear JAWS at all. So I said to Orell, 'You know what, hold the headphones. From now on I am going to be the mic person.'
>
> This was the night that I decided I was gonna use the name DJ Cane. That name had been given to me about two weeks before by a brother called Beenie. I always try to talk like people on the radio because my main thing was to get into radio; I wanted to get into radio. So this was my opportunity. Some of my friends who came

that night didn't believe it was me on the mic. Everyone was asking 'Who is that on the mic?' They just didn't believe.

As technology evolved, DJ Cane endeavoured to remain relevant. He read voraciously which positioned him to update the software he used. So when he learned about Mixxx in 2012, he did not hesitate to find out about this cutting-edge programme. He explained, "This is a DJ software and it is easy for blind people to use. I became a full-fledged DJ. I sat up night after night, day after day, practising my mixing. I felt like YES! Mi reach now!"

Cane did not choose to operate as the average practitioner. He tried to equip himself to ensure he remained a major player in the industry. First, he had started with VLC and Windows Media Player, then he graduated to Mixxx and subsequently learned of GoldWave. This is editing software that helps the user to eliminate all flaws and add creativity to the production. Quickly, he sought to master this in an effort to enrich his output which helped tremendously to boost the quality of his production.

In 2015 he was asked to play on an online radio station. This request emanated from his vast knowledge of music and the industry, and his willingness to share. His friends would often call him with questions and often he would be recommended to students who were working on projects and needed information on the history of music. He recalls:

A friend of mine was going to UWI at the time and he introduced me to one of his friends called Orane who was doing a course and wanted songs that would complement his topic. So, for example, if he was doing something on female abuse, he would call me, and I would just give him some songs off the bat that he could use. So from then, he was very impressed with my knowledge of the music and how quickly I could find songs to fit [a given] situation.

In 2015 now, he linked me up saying, 'Listen, I want to do internet radio and you're knowledgeable of the music. I don't know yet if you are a DJ or what, but I want to give you a two-hour slot on the radio station to do whatever you want to do.'

I explained to him that I now had the software that I could use to record and do my mixing. But I could not take up the offer at the time as my laptop was giving some trouble. A few weeks later, he called me up again, asking me if I no longer wanted the opportunity and I told him I was ready now as I got my laptop sorted out.

Two days after he called me, I had my show ready for him.

So now I am a full-fledged DJ on ZANJ Radio. *You can visit us. My programme is called 'Musical Altitude'. [It] gives you a higher education in music as I will give you a little history here and there. So it's a high elevation music mix, hence the name Musical Altitude.*

DJ Cane explains that this online radio programme has won him many international fans, and even clients, as he has had people make requests to purchase some of his shows.

It is natural for persons with disabilities to go through particular phases in their careers where they perhaps need to work three times as hard as others to get where they want to be. In other words, the doubts and scepticism surrounding our abilities are palpable – resulting from the negative attitudinal barriers that exist in society towards persons with disabilities (Oliver 1990) and, as a consequence, these individuals have to demonstrate their efficacy as postulated by Bandura (1986). DJ Cane, for instance, argues that in the initial stage of his career, though he is very appreciative of the experiences, he volunteered most of his time. "Like any other thing that a blind person is going into, you won't earn at the outset," he says, "meaning, people want to see what you can do first and then they'll decide say yes, dem ago pay yuh fi do it. So, in the past I had to do a lot of free shows."

Regarding the various aspects of his work, he says, "I think differently with the playing and the disc jockey thing out there, I think it's a lot kinder to you than the building of riddims [beats]. I think people who want you to play music are more willing to pay. I have observed that. For me, right now I think this is where I make a good portion of my small earnings."

DJ Cane's plan is to create some mixes, place them on CDs and issue them as a means of promotion of his work. He is also promoting his online programme to increase his fan base with the hope that he will get more clients who would be interested in purchasing his shows. Moreover, he has been the resident DJ for the "Entertainment Trail", a live show aired on News Talk 93 FM, on a Saturday from 4:00 p.m. to 6:00 p.m., since 2015.

Admirers

The indefatigable, industrious and affable Damion "DJ Cane" Rose continues to attract more and more admirers. With his meticulous attention to detail, his inexorable pursuit of excellence and his vivacious and infectious high spirit, this visually impaired musician inspires and impresses several persons with whom he works. Renowned reggae artiste and attorney-at-law, Charles "Advoket" Gangasingh, notes that DJ Cane provided the drumbeats for three of his songs:

> *DJ Cane's contribution was significant as drumbeats are key to the embellishment of any song. With Rose, there is no room for mediocrity; he sets his sights on the production of high quality output, and has an admirable work ethic. He has a keen ear for the optimum. I would recommend DJ Cane to everyone in the music industry who needs drumbeats in a song.*

Founder and chief executive officer of ZANJ Radio, Orrin Kerr, shares similar sentiments:

> *His drumbeats are of exceptional quality. DJ Cane has been working with the radio station for the past five-and-a-half years in the capacity of presenter and producer as well as a sound editor. He dedicates much of his energy, time and knowledge in maintaining the elevated output of this station. He is extremely talented at what he does. He is an affable person, easy to work with and very knowledgeable within his field of music. He is also very diligent and respectable.*

DJ Cane's disposition towards work belies his lack of sight. Advoket attests to this: "DJ Cane's greatest asset is his behaviour. He acts as if he hasn't lost his sight. If one were to sit and talk with [him], one would not be aware that [he] has any visual impairment." Kerr concurs, "DJ Cane's disability does not alter his high quality performance in anyway. Quite the contrary, I think he uses his physical limitation to his advantage."

A person's physical challenge is not a deterrent to maximum performance as demonstrated by Damion "DJ Cane" Rose. When asked his views on the treatment of persons with disabilities in Jamaica as it pertains to work, Kerr laments that they are not given equal opportunity in this country. "In general, Jamaica is not as friendly or accommodating to persons with disabilities as we would like." However, he expresses a no-bar policy at his online radio station: "We at ZANJ Radio try to ensure that we play our part in remedying such discriminatory maladies, so that we can have healthy and motivating relationships that stimulate us to create and produce the best content related to our objectives within the Jamaican creative cultural industry." On this issue, Gangasingh feels that to prejudge anyone because he or she has some physical limitations is tantamount to fuelling the beast of discrimination: a monster which continues to plague the lives of countless people living with physical challenges in this country. Discrimination is a social construct that serves to isolate and restrict the effective participation of persons with impairments on an equal basis with others (Oliver 1990).

Evidently, Damion "DJ Cane" Rose has proved that no physical limitation can restrict his prowess. His exemplary performance as a musician, presenter and producer has demonstrated to those with whom he works that with strict adherence to discipline, dedication and the maintenance of the highest standards of professionalism, one can readily overcome and eclipse the expectations of others, especially one's detractors.

Damion Rose continues to display that despite having a disability, he can achieve excellence in his pursuits. Through hard work and discipline and love for music, he has managed to carve out a niche in the music industry and is making a signal contribution to the cultural advancement of Jamaica. He is undoubtedly a music and entertainment ambassador for persons with disabilities and, by extension, for Jamaica. He might lack sight, but he has vision.

Derrick Morgan:
The Birth of a Legend

Gather together, be brothers and sisters
We're independent, we're independent
Join hands to hands, children started to dance
We're independent, we're independent

Don't be sad and blue, the Lord is still with you
Because the time has come when you can have your fun
So make a run, we're independent

Brothers and sisters, give joy and praises
While it's under, yeah, yeah
Brothers and sisters, give joy and praise
To His commandments, yeah, yeah

Don't be sad and blue, the Lord is still with you
Because the time has come when you can have your fun
So make a run, yeah, yeah.

(Derrick Morgan 1962)

Another legend in Jamaica's cultural industry is Derrick Morgan, a person who is blind who has been an ambassador for music.

Derrick Morgan's emergence on the music scene can be compared to the hewing of a rough-cut diamond from the remote hillside of Mocho, Clarendon, where he was born. Over time, the diamond would be honed, polished and fashioned to perfection. The first three years of his life were spent in this close-knit village with his aunt, who detected that there were problems with Morgan's sight. At that young and sensitive stage of his life, he was sent to reside with his mother in Kingston where he was later diagnosed with retina pigmentation, a hereditary degenerative disease of the eye, which would eventually claim his sight.

During his formative years, there was evidence of a sparkle emanating from this uncut diamond as Morgan's father, a deacon in the local church, lured his son into the choir. His educational journey began at the Allman Town Elementary School in Kingston, continued at Kingston Senior, and ended at the Model Private School in the same parish.

Setting the Foot to the Path

In 1957, a watershed year in colonial Jamaica, when the island was granted self-government by its colonial masters, the British, the genuine brilliance of this diamond became evident. Morgan exploded on the scene. That year he entered and won a popular talent competition, the Vere John's Opportunity Hour. Among his rivals in the contest were emerging artistes like Jackie Edwards, Eric "Monty" Morris, Hortense Ellis, and Owen Gray, who later became kingpins themselves in the Jamaican music industry. In the competition, Morgan reeled off popular songs of the day like "Long Tall Sally" and "Jenny", current and trendy Rock and Roll favourites by Little Richard whom Morgan impersonated quite well. As a rising star, he embarked on an island-wide tour with the twin comedians Bim and Bam – which added significantly to his burgeoning popularity.

However, his professional career did not begin until 1959 when he met the iconic producer Duke Reid. It was during that year under the majestic wings of Reid that Morgan released his debut hits "Loverboy" and "Oh My". Reid discovered Morgan during an earnest quest for young and dynamic talent for his Treasure Isle record label. Anecdotally, it was alleged that Reid was a gunslinger who strolled around with two guns. If things were not going his way during recordings, it was said that Reid would "let it rip", and people would get the clear and unambiguous message. Morgan asserts that Reid's intimidation of musicians and artistes contributed largely to the high quality of his productions. Derrick also recorded with legendary producer Clement "Sir Coxsone" Dodd, another giant in the field of music production in the land of ska.

During the 1960s Derrick was in his element and achieved the unprecedented feat of having the top seven songs on the national pop singles chart. In the country's rich and varied musical history no artiste has since reached such dizzying heights. In fact, this commanding figure captured the attention of every imaginable lover of music in the 1960s and was justifiably crowned the "King of Ska" during that era. Among his memorable chart-toppers in 1960 were "Be Still", "In My Heart", "Don't Call Me Daddy", "Moon Hop", and "Meekly Wait and Murmur Not".

Morgan's dominance continued unabated as the following year saw him release his number one song of all-time, "Housewives' Choice", which featured Millicent "Patsy" Todd. As a consequence of the large number of requests the song was receiving on radio, it was renamed "You Don't Know How Much I Love You" by broadcaster Marie Garth, and his epic and unstoppable march on the path of success continued.

In 1962, the year of Jamaica's political independence, the icon again broke new ground as he produced the first song in celebration of this momentous milestone. The song, "Forward March" helped to instil a great sense of hope in the breast of every living Jamaican. Moreover, it inspired vigour, hope and new possibilities in the hearts of a people who held high and proud dreams for a newly born country.

Derrick Morgan, true pioneer and a patriarch of Jamaican music, started yet another trend unknown to the Jamaican music industry at the time – feuding, where there was consistent and intense competition and rivalry between two artistes. His arch rival was Prince Buster whose career Morgan had shepherded. According to him, the "musical war" began in 1962 when he recorded "Forward March". He recalls that Prince Buster had maintained that the singer had taken part of his song, "They Got to Come", and as a result, felt cheated. This epic battle between the two only served to heighten the country's interest in the music. Also, the rivalry witnessed the churning out of more quality hits from them both. During this musical war, both artistes produced hits including Morgan's "Blazing Fire" and "Blackhead Chiney". The ferocity of the competition spiralled. During the period, both artistes gained much popularity and each had a great number of followers who claimed that one or the other of the artistes was better. The dispute reached the extent where the government became concerned about the uproar, and in 1962, they were both called by the Bustamante-led government to create an image of unity as the fans of the artistes were now involved in heated rivalry.

Sounds familiar? Only a few years ago, popular dancehall artistes Vybz Kartel and Mavado were summoned by the government of the day to Jamaica House in a bid to quell a rising musical feud between supporters of the artistes which threatened to get out of control. The two talented artistes had divided dancehall supporters into two distinct camps: Gaza which supports Vybz Kartel, and Gully which supports Mavado. The division was so intense that then Prime Minister Bruce Golding led the intervention with the two artistes. Emanating from the discussion, it was agreed to have graffiti that were painted about the artistes removed and for a peace concert to be held with both camps (*Jamaica Gleaner* 2009).

Governmental interventions in the musical feuds in Jamaica demonstrate the extent of the socio-political effect of the artistes on the population. The citizens see themselves as a part of the artiste's network and will go the extra mile to demonstrate their support. Sometimes this passion manifests itself in violence in communities. Usually, the Government of Jamaica would recognize this nexus and potential social disorder and therefore intervene as a preventative strategy.

Further Glory

Although visually impaired, Derrick Morgan did not allow this impediment to hamper or deter his relentless progress. He continued to create gigantic waves throughout a fledgling music industry in Jamaica, and as it evolved from one era to another Morgan scored many firsts.

He was among the first artistes to make a rocksteady hit, "Tougher Than Tough". Another hit, "Went to the Hop", was the first Jamaican music production with the employment of the electric bass guitar. His accomplishments continued to increase as "Blazing Fire" was the first local song to use an electric piano. "Love Not to Brag" is credited as the first Jamaican duet with a female artiste, Millicent "Patsy" Todd, and "Seven Letters" is thought to be the first reggae song produced in collaboration with brother-in-law Bunny Lee. "Fat Man" became one of the first Jamaican records ever issued in the United Kingdom and became an instant hit both there and in Jamaica where it topped the local charts. "Housewives' Choice" is regarded as one of the overall bestselling West Indian records in the United Kingdom and it is believed that it would have made the charts if the BBC had registered sales in specialist outlets.

Morgan did not only contribute as an artiste to the music industry. He produced music for the great Bob Marley, the legendary Jimmy Cliff, and Garnet Silk.

In recent times, he has put pen to paper contributing to the age-old Festival Song competition in Jamaica. Among his winning compositions were "Jamaica Whoa" performed by Neville Martin in 1998; Stanley Beckford's "Fi Wi Island a Boom" in 2000; and in 2002 Devon Black sang another winner, "Progress".

Yet the ska king refuses to quit. Morgan has performed in many shows, and according to Kool FM broadcaster Michael Barnett, continues to mesmerize fans with his dulcet tones. In 2002, in Ontario, Canada there was a reunification of the ska legends. This featured the Skatalites, Lloyd Brevett, Lester Sterling, and Morgan himself. In 2007 Morgan appeared on the bill at the annual Augustibuller music festival in Sweden. His song, "Tougher Than Tough", was featured in the video game "Scarface: The World Is Yours". Even more recently he headlined the Supernova International Ska Festival in Fredericksburg, Virginia in 2017.

Morgan Speaks

In a recent interview with Xavier Murphy of Jamaica.com, Morgan, while revelling in being referred to as the "King of Ska", noted that, "The face of ska has really changed. Most of the leading ska music today comes from the white bands. There are quite a few good ones out there like 'Bad Manners' [out of London] and 'Rude Rich and the High Notes' [from Amsterdam]." In describing his journey, he said:

> I started singing at age 14 at a school contest. I made my public debut at 17. The very song I recorded was 'Lover Boy' which was also known as 'Scorchers Rap'. I recorded that song with Duke Reid. Back then there was only one recording studio in the island. It was called Federal. I have recorded about 24 albums of my own and lots of combinations with other artists.

Derrick Morgan acknowledged that Little Richard was his greatest influence and went on to identify those whom he considers the unsung heroes of the ska era. He says, "Theophilus Beckford was never really recognized for his contributions. I also think Eric "Monty" Morris never got his dues."

But there are many other artistes who he listed as having captured his admiration during the evolution of the music: "In the early ska days I liked Toots and the Maytals. In the rocksteady era I liked Ken Boothe. In the early reggae days I liked Beres Hammond. Today I like Beenie Man, Popcaan, Buju Banton, and Chaka Demus and Pliers." When asked about the sound system that he enjoyed in the early days he revealed, "V-Rocket was my favourite sound system. They used to play all nice songs. The best DJ back then was known as Machukia. He was really good and used to ride a donkey and dress like Jesus when he entered the dance. King Stitchie and Coxsone were also good in those days."

He points out that the "toasting" of Jamaican DJs is largely responsible for the advent of rap music and credits Daddy U-Roy for his significant contribution in this respect. His own contribution can be affirmed by the fact that people in the industry have sought his advice on the renaissance of ska among reggae artistes: "Buju's promoters had contacted me a while back to do collaboration. Some of them call me for advice. One of the problems I have is I don't like the chord rhythm they are using. I like changes, and need good background music. This is why I have not done any recent collaboration."

Appreciation

Acclaimed reggae singer Queen Ifrica, his daughter, says that though her early childhood was not spent with her father, she attributes her love and passion for the music to him and does not feel that Morgan is recognized enough for his vast contribution to Jamaican reggae. She lauds him for his deep fervour and enthusiasm for the music, and for his clinical precision in executing his duties. She regards him as the consummate professional which she connects to his lack of sight: "Daddy does not see, therefore, he utilizes his keen hearing when it comes to the music. This is a skill that is sadly lacking among some artistes these days." Youth in the business, she argues, could learn much from him, noting that the great Bob Marley benefited tremendously from his wealth of knowledge.

She links Morgan's longevity to his adherence to better health practices in recent times, and thinks that his spiritual outlook also helps to keep him strong even in his late 70s. This star in the music industry views Morgan's ability to detect quality output as a hallmark of his remarkable success over the years. She remarks on his mastery of different genres, and commends him for it. Queen

Ifrica has shared the stage with Morgan in recent times, and shows like Heineken Star Time and tours of Europe have provided these opportunities. According to her, "This has given me the chance to get closer to him, and get to know him far better." She discloses that a collaboration with him is in the pipeline.

Another icon, Dennis "Alcapone" Smith, dates his association with Morgan from the early 1960s, but says his love and appreciation for Morgan's music go back even further. He says Morgan "ruled the roost" in the 60s, and he was one of his greatest fans. Their working relationship only began in the 1980s where both he and Morgan worked on the national independence festival and other shows. Both artistes collaborated on one of Morgan's myriad hits, "Fatman", done at Dynamic Studio and produced by Lynford Anderson, known as "Andy Capp". During their working relationship, Alcapone says their friendship mushroomed and, in fact, Morgan was responsible for introducing him to Bunny "Striker" Lee who became his producer for many years. "I think that his unique voice, lyrical content and his ability to churn out hit after hit were his strong points."

Alcapone considers the rivalry between Prince Buster and Morgan was fodder for his amazing creativity. According to Alcapone, Morgan's "Forward March", which was in part the genesis of the rivalry, helped significantly to boost his image among the public back then. He argues that these present-day youth could emulate the love and passion that Morgan displayed for the music. This, he contends, would assist them greatly in moving the music forward as, "their greed and hunger for the mighty dollar only mashing up di music". Alcapone links the high standard of the music in the 60s to the commitment of artistes like Morgan. He views Morgan's ability to string hits together with alarming frequency as one of his greatest legacies. He laments the falling standards of the music today.

In conclusion, Derrick Morgan's high standards, quality music, and dynamism have contributed to his longevity and the recognition of the true champion he has become over time. His tremendous legacy will never be altered. After 50 years he has definitely etched an indelible imprint in the minds of all music lovers. Irrespective of his visual disability, he demonstrates that you can be at the top of your game if you believe in yourself and place an intrinsic value on quality. Morgan's immense contribution to Jamaica's culture is a vindication of the arguments postulated by Oliver (1990) that it is social barriers that restrict the equal participation and inclusion in society of persons with impairments. If these barriers are eradicated, the talents and abilities of individuals like Morgan will become efficacious (Bandura 1986).

It is incumbent upon the powers that be to ensure that Morgan is given the long overdue recognition he deserves. Despite his limitations, he has torn down barriers for many artistes, even those who have gone on to even greater acknowledgement than he has had. Morgan has taken the music far and wide and contributed to Jamaica's global recognition as a musical superpower. He is undoubtedly one of Jamaica's finest musicians and has contributed immensely to the country's music and entertainment industry.

Latifa Brown: aka "Tifa" – The Certified Diva

Mi a di b-a-d-d-e-s-t
A gal caan chat cause she l-a-m-e
Dem a p-r-e dem caan be m-e
Cause mi done have the city well l-o-c-k

A wah do d-e-m
A wah do baby shrek an har pop dung fren
Fava duppy night a di d-e-a-d
Dem betta gwaan guh gully creeper like i-c-e

R-I-P mi boss straight to di fullest
But some gal a hype an dem inna m-e-s-s
Dem a beat dem chest bout who a di bess
An dem full a s-t-r-e-s-s

(Latifa Brown 2009)

Latifa Brown was born with a physical disability that impeded her ability to walk properly. Despite this impediment, she has become one of the dominant female dancehall artistes, well recognized locally and internationally.

Life poses many challenges. However, the will to be steadfast and persevere through these trials is a marked accomplishment. Latifa Brown was born on December 12, 1983 in Kingston, Jamaica. Known in many circles of the entertainment and cultural industry as "Tifa", she can truly be described as a real dream chaser. While still a young girl, her parents separated. Her grandmother, now her legal guardian, offered emotional support as her mother migrated to the United States and provided for her material needs. Latifa visited her during the long holidays which somewhat compensated for her daily physical absence.

Brown's grandmother owned a restaurant and bar where Tifa developed an appreciation and relish for local music. There she started singing and dancing, as she discovered that she had an amazing talent for both. She attended Wolmer's Girls Preparatory School where she excelled at academics, and her talent in the arts was nurtured and encouraged through her participation in the dance club, drama, and the school choir. Her ambitious spirit was fuelled further by early contests with her cousin, as both often competed against each other in dance and singing.

Despite early signs of talent in dance, Brown was impacted by a physical disability. At birth she was diagnosed with Blount's disease, a growth disorder that affects the bones of the lower limbs causing them to bow outward. Tifa had to undergo three surgeries which were necessary to correct her inability to walk properly.

In an interview with the *Gleaner* published on February 20, 2017 she disclosed that a scorpion had stung her pregnant mother in the area of her navel, and this poison was transferred to her foetus, poisoning the unformed bones. Her mother's lack of appetite also resulted in her imbibing insufficient minerals and vitamins for strong and healthy bones (*Jamaica Gleaner* 2017a).

Latifa sat the entrance examination for matriculation into high school, and although she was hospitalized when she received the results, her discomfort was eased somewhat by the joy of acquiring a place at Wolmer's High School for Girls.

For the first two years of high school Tifa was in a cast and wheel-chair. As a result she was unable to participate in sports and one of her favourite art forms, dancing. By this time her grandmother had died and her mother had returned to Jamaica. Her inability to participate in sports and dancing at the time was as a result of environmental and attitudinal barriers that restrict the participa-tion of individuals with impairment in society on an equal basis with others (Oliver 1990). Most of the educational institutions in Jamaica are not equipped with the requisite facilities to maximize the full potential of persons with disabilities (Morris 2017; Gayle-Geddes 2015).

Fortunately, by the end of second form, she was able to move about freely and after successfully auditioning for the group, imme-diately became a member of Ashe, a performing arts ensemble, where she remained for six years. She quickly became famous on both the entertainment and sports scenes as she was not only an entertainer, but also a leading goaltender in hockey.

Many persons think that children with disabilities ought to be confined indoors and that their lives should be limited. Society has set up diverse restrictions for these people and this has contributed to most of them not being able to maximize their talents. However, Tifa has defied the odds and proved that your abilities are not determined by your impairment, but rather by the amount of will power you expend to propel yourself forward. Tifa says:

> At home I didn't know I was different until I went to school or went out and people are like 'Look, look', or whatever. But I wasn't made to feel different. I always had friends at school and they were taught not to tease or anything, I know something was different but I don't feel different. And you see my mom enrolled me in everything. [She was] like, 'Okay, so you want to dance? Okay, you are going to dancing. Okay, so you want to do acting? Okay, you are going to do acting. You want to play hockey? Okay, you can play hockey.' She pushed me to do extracurricular stuff to build me.

This is what Bandura (1986) points to as necessary to build success and efficacy of persons with disabilities.

Tifa was offered a hockey scholarship to study abroad, however, she had plans to study locally, so she turned it down. She then attended The University of the West Indies (UWI) where she completed her major in psychology and her minor in human resource management and was awarded her BSc degree. Tifa recalled that while she was at The UWI she would sense that people had an interest in her, but as soon as they discovered that she had a physical disability, they lost interest. She recounts: "I remember sitting in KFC and a guy coming to talk to me, and me getting up to throw something in the bin and him just get up, like, 'Okay, she cute but har foot dem nuh so cute; so I'm a bounce.'"

Destined for Greatness

The Ashe ensemble started in 1993 with the objective of preserving Jamaican/Afro-Caribbean culture and creating social change amongst youth through the use of entertainment. Tifa joined the group at age 12, with her raw talent. In the six years she spent with the company she developed professionalism and toured Jamaica, the United States and the Caribbean. She says:

Mommy started to enrol me into groups and the first time I really realized I wanted to do this is when I joined that company, Ashe. And perhaps the first time I got my real solo – because, you know you have to work for your solos, because it's like hundreds of kids and everybody wants it; and it's the best of the best... I think it's the first time I got my real solo, I got a standing ovation. And it was a wow for me... it gave me such empowerment. It went from 'there goes the bend-foot girl' [to commendation]... then I realized I could do something beyond my legs, and people appreciated and recognized that.

These are the self-efficacy and motivational factors that Bandura (1986) speaks about. Parents must rally around their children with disabilities and have them integrated into mainstream activities. Strong parental support plus self-motivation are paramount to the success of persons with disabilities (Morris 2017).

The touring exposure was beneficial, as she was now introduced to a wider market and was later able to venture out as a solo artiste. In an interview with London-based Boomshot TV, she shared her view that it was her love and commitment towards music, the support from her mother and the will she had to excel that motivated her belief in herself and exploded into the success she was experiencing then. As Tifa became more ingrained into the music industry, she quickly developed a huge fan base for herself. On the other hand, detractors also emerged. Negative rumours were circulated and eventually, she began to experience discrimination as a result of her physical disability and the appearance of her legs. Some persons showed prejudice against her because of her lighter skin colour and others did not see the need for an individual with a degree to be positioned in the dancehall space. She explained:

A lot of people are offended by these [making reference to her feet]; a lot of people are offended by me, and not because I have necessarily done anything to them. Like for example, somebody once said 'Nuff dark-skin woman did a do dancehall long before and them chose to put a light-skin uptown handicap gyal pon a billboard.'

Nonetheless, she had a robustly confident mother, and this, along with her own mental solidity pulled her through all the turmoil intended to daunt her spirit. She told Boomshot TV:

You know, you have those dense people that are very judgemental;

and I think even now, especially in dancehall, that's a hurdle I had to cross. 'Cause initially that's what they saw, like, 'Oh she too cute to do dancehall'; or 'Oh, har leg them, nuh body naa go really . . .' I had to push three hundred times harder, not only as a woman but somebody that they saw [negatively]. 'Okay, you have a degree; so somebody with a degree does dancehall? So somebody that lives where she lives does dancehall? So somebody that walks the way she walks does dancehall?' So I had to break that barrier down; and a lot of people in the industry are surprised at where I am today, and I think that's what caught everybody off guard. But I am here. That's all that matters.

Many were critical as it was not their belief that she really deserved such a prominent spotlight; some believed that she operated through the links of her stepfather (producer Garfield "Sampalue" Phillips); others believed she used the payola system; and being a female, there were those who concluded that she was involved with many producers, promoters and or disc jocks. None of these rumours were ever proven to be true. Covetousness or "badminded-ness" is a strong feature in the dancehall space in Jamaica and this seems to best explain what Latifa was experiencing.

Though Tifa's first single to be fully recognized was "Spell It Out", at the time she found it very difficult to be admitted into the business. The song got a lot of airplay but her listeners did not really know her. It was not until she signed an endorsement deal with telecommunication company Digicel that persons were now able to match the face with the voice, and this was the break that her career needed. Tifa has released one album, *Curry Goat and Champagne*, and several hit songs and musical projects over the years.

Through her prolific music career, she has done works with artistes such as Spice, Wayne Marshall, Fambo, Dexta Daps, and Khalia, and worked with producers and labels such as Ward 21, Washroom Entertainment, Christopher Birch, and Di Genius Records. For her studio album she worked with Lee Milla Productions on the lead track. Her hit singles include "Spell It Out" (2009), "Move Yuh Body" (2010), "Matey Wine" (2011), "Big Bumper" (2016), and "Hype Doh Pay My Bills" (2017).

In yet another hit, "Overcome", Tifa speaks out against members of the industry or persons in general who seem to be seeking her demise – "Dem neva tink mi woulda de yah, watch me now... all dem try fi fight and conquer, mi stronger now."

The lyrics demonstrate that although Tifa has been in the industry for a long time, she acknowledges that discrimination and envy are still part of her journey. For anyone to make it in the music industry, one has to be of strong character and have the mental fortitude to stand up to anything, more so if you are a person with a disability.

Ashe Director Michael Holgate who has been part of the company from its start, and who experienced working with little Latifa Brown, strongly believes that Tifa has contributed in many areas to Jamaica's culture and spoke highly of her:

Tifa was well received in the Ashe Company. As a member of the Ashe Academy over numerous years, she was greatly loved because she had such a beautiful personality – full of fun and vibe and energy. In addition to that, Ashe has always been about talent maximization and empowerment. Our policy supports all persons and is non-discriminatory.

It was easy to love her, because she gave so much of herself in every moment, both on and off the stage. It was also very easy to love her mother, who was greatly supportive and always around. I have never seen a more committed and dedicated mother.

Tifa was a great inspiration to her fellow Ashe Academy members and also to the more seasoned ensemble performing group for various reasons. Her talent was obvious and it shone. She was recognized most as a singer – she has a beautiful singing voice. She was an energetic dancer who again was not afraid to take risks. 'Fearless' must have been her middle name from even then. She allowed no one to think of her as different, not because of what she said, but because of how she operated.

She is a powerfully self-motivated, brilliantly creative and fearless artiste. It takes a lot of will power to become an artiste under any condition. In Jamaica it requires a kind of stamina and mental fortitude that is not easy to come by. For a female artiste it takes even more, because the music industry seems to favour the development of male artistes. For someone who is all of the above and also has a physical challenge that is limiting, it is that much more difficult, and yet Tifa rose to such great heights as a Jamaican female DJ. That is not accidental. She is powerful. She is wise beyond her years and she is beautiful. The beauty is soul deep as much as it is also physical.

Tifa brought back a kind of lyrical genius to the dancehall genre when she did 'Spell It Out'. She is also an excellent performer who knows how to communicate with her audience and a responsible role model for young girls. She is an inspiration to all.

Suku, a member of Ward 21 (a group of dancehall musicians and producers), shared his experience of what it was like to work with Tifa for over 10 years. From the outset, he saw her as a talented and passionate artiste with good work ethics. He recalls that throughout his work with her, she released quite a few collaborations which he confirmed were well received. These included "Crawny Gal", "Spell It Out", "Tinky Winky" featuring Timberlee, "Best Friend", "Bottom of the Barrel", and more. Suku proposes that other artistes should possess passion in what they do and foster good work ethics.

At the start of her career when she had to undergo surgery related to her disability, it must have been an immense challenge for the vivacious Latifa Brown to transition into a more relaxed way of life as she recuperated. However, the process was facilitated by the excellent love, compassion and encouragement she received from her mother and well-wishers. Strong consistent parental support and encouragement are inestimable ingredients for the success of a person with a disability. Love and motivation contribute to great accomplishments.

Tifa was raised to believe that she could achieve any goal she wanted in life and there were no limits placed on her. She therefore went about life taking positive risks and committing her time and talents towards her greater goals. Many believe in her because of her rich talent and others believe in her because of her thirst and hunger for success. All these coupled with her vision, allow her to continuously press forward. Tifa is still living the life of a true overcomer and persists in working harder to go even farther with her career. She has demonstrated that in order to maintain focus on one's dream, one must avoid naysayers, as they may draw you into their negativity and cause you to lose out. Her positive outlook has made Tifa a force to be reckoned with in the music industry, and she has contributed considerably to the development of Jamaica's culture through music and entertainment.

Peter Clarke and Devon Palmer

Two mega-talented persons with visual disabilities who have contributed to the advancement of Jamaica's culture are Peter Clarke and Devon Palmer. Though their careers are separate, both have played in several musical bands and have indelibly stamped their mark on the music industry.

Peter Clarke

Born in the parish of Clarendon, Peter came from a family of music lovers. But it was not until he attended the Salvation Army School for the Blind and Visually Impaired where he joined the school choir that he also became involved with music. He started in the choir and was a committed member, but found that his interest lay more in the sound and the compilation of the beat rather than in the lyrical content of the music. With this realization came the decision to learn to play an instrument instead of singing. Clarke says: "I started music at a tender age at the School for the Blind, but it goes way beyond that. I had an uncle called Texas Ranger who used to play on a sound system – as he still does. Through him I fell in love with the riddim aspect of the music."

It was his music teacher at the School for the Blind who taught him his first musical note, and was integral in his honing of his musical skills. According to Peter: "I started to sing on the school choir from the infant block [and continued] to the senior level. Ms Sheila James was our music teacher and mi always hear some nice sound a come out of her room. I said to myself, mi must learn dah something yah. But how?"

Peter and his friends decided they needed to come up with a good plan to learn to play a keyboard. At that time they were not allowed to just sit down and play as they wished, so they decided they were going to wait until no one was around and make best use of the unauthorized opportunity. However, as soon as they started to use the keyboard, they were caught. Peter was nevertheless determined that he would learn to play music. When Ms James realized his hunger, she decided to teach him. Although he was eager to practise daily, Ms James was not always available and as a result Peter wasn't learning as quickly as he wanted. He recalls:

> *The first note Ms James taught me was C Major, but because of the heavy amount of students she had per day she didn't have time to sit down with me every evening. So I started to understand the thing [on my own] and [my knowledge] started to multiply. I started to understand the rules of the music and [learned] the scales; and [learned] that the same [rules applied], high or low.*

Peter eventually developed his craft and started playing keyboard at devotion and other services at school. His knowledge of the music business was further developed under the tutelage of Fab 5 and Unique Vision bands, and under their guidance he really started to understand the craft of the musical engineer. "Then and there mi learn the whole thing about engineering, how you mix band, the different sounds of how a band put together, how music put together to get certain sounds and them neva run mi out a dem studio yet. Dem teach mi things."

Getting Ready for Nine-Night

In his last year of school he was part of the group that entered the "Teen Star Search" competition. The exposure and experience he acquired during this process really caused his career to explode. For the first time ever, his school reached the finals in the competition and it was because people loved his DJ voice. Following on from that, Peter worked steadily in the business until he started playing for churches. Many of them came and asked him to play at their events, then he moved on to playing at "Nine-Nights". This is a cultural practice, a wake, where traditionally communities would gather at the home on the ninth night after someone had died to sing songs, play games (mostly dominoes), and eat food in celebration of the life of the deceased. More recently these activities have started to feature live bands which accompany the singing and perform while people dance. This is where Peter found his place in the industry. He started working with Phillip and Sons, a band in Clarendon, where demand for his talent grew significantly:

Bands start hear bout me, schools, business... and now the whole business of Nine-Night came about, where people nuh sing and knock [dominoes] round table nuh more. People a hire bands fi come a Nine-Night. So that is a major break out fi mi now. I... worked with Phillip and Sons... for 16 years straight and mi a tell yuh seh a nuh-nuh easy music. Wi just a 'shot' the place. I also worked with Whitter and Son for six years and am still with them.

Soon Peter's playing was so infectious that people would stand for no other band at their relative's Nine-Night.

Supreme

In 2013 Peter and his wife started their own band called Supreme. He surmises that even though there is room for expansion, the level which they have attained ensures their customer base is large because of the appreciation people have for their music. Currently Supreme entertains across the island: "We go out on a weekly basis to hotels, resorts, church functions, and other events."

The band consists of two singers and three musicians including Peter. Good customer service is vital in any business. It is what makes customers consistently come to an individual or organization to acquire goods and services. For Peter, he is constantly working to improve in an attempt to continuously satisfy his audience, which will in turn satisfy his clients. Peter is looking to enhance the sound of his band in order to boost their unique standing in the market. "The plan for the band going forward is that there are some things... that we need to upgrade. As you know, the sound quality is really important, so we really going to add some more power equipment. The cleaner your equipment, the more people willing to pay."

Though Peter is visually impaired, he was inspired by music and that drove him to want to learn more about music, so he would be able to play on his own. Today he is seen as a veteran in the music industry. He is loved by many and still continues to entertain and satisfy his clients. He shared his observations:

My disability make me multitask cause I usually service my own equipment. My disability for people right now is like a show, cause people come roun and a ask mi, 'You can't see good so how yuh si fi do this?' But whatever I put my hand to it is well done, so people always a ask.

Devon Palmer

The owner of two bands, Devon believes that he and music were destined to be together – a match made in heaven which became evident while he was a student at the Salvation Army School for the Blind and Visually Impaired.

I began making music from the School for the Blind in Ms James' class and she taught me music. From I was at the school, I figured out that music was the best thing to do for me because it is a gift. From Ms James taught me the basics of it, is like everything just come together. So it is a good way out.

He flirted with the idea of a nine-to-five job for a brief moment, but his heart was never in it.

I also used to do other things. I used to work at Alma Jones Medical Centre down there on Hagley Park Road. It was not a good thing; meaning that you wake up, you leave to go to work, you spend all day at work come back 7 [o'clock] and is like all your day gone. I needed something more meaningful. So that is the reason why I chose music.

This bold decision paid off. When Devon left school, he started working with the Optic Revolution band under the guidance of Roy Dunbar. He was then introduced to Ainsley Morris who had a successful band on the North Coast. This proved to be the fuel this "vehicle" needed as it was there that his musical career was launched and he has not looked back. Contracted to work at the renowned Bahia Principe hotel in St Ann, Palmer owns and operates two bands: a reggae band and a steel band. He notes:

For the reggae band there is a drum, keyboard, bass guitar, the singer, and the horn section, and I play the percussion. For the steel band now, we have three members who play pan – two double seconds and a bass player – plus a normal bass guitarist, and the drummer which is me.

According to him, these bands perform as often as four to five times per week, and this has been happening since the opening of the hotel more than 15 years ago. This is testament to their good work as they are the resident band and the first to be called whenever there is an important function scheduled.

We play for the weddings and functions. Say, for example, there are sometimes two weddings a day. Whenever there is a wedding that entails a steel band or a reggae band we play. So we might play maybe say, five times for the week with the steel band and three times per month for the reggae band.

Contrary to what many believe, Palmer thinks that music requires much more research than that which meets the eye. This is especially so when performing on the hotel circuit. One must have a lucid understanding of what the clients need, and this can only be had through research.

Your band have to be somebody who really know music. And know how to select the music by the mood of the people. Because you can go on a stage and say we are going to play 'That Girl', and we are going to play Dennis Brown and all of that... Freddy MacGregor; but no you can't do that. You have to look at the mood of the people and [then] you select. Then you will get people involved and start to dance to what you are singing. Sometimes the crowd is very hard to figure out but most of the times – 98 per cent – we have them figured out. You have to know the country the people come from; you have to know the language they speak; and you have to know the age group, to select your songs. [Success] is just based on the selection.

The pressure placed on them to play certain music can be overbearing sometimes and one has to know how to deal with these challenges. Not all songs can be played when requested based on the environment and audience. Devon remembers one particular incident while on stage when undue pressure to play a particular song was placed on them:

I remember once we were playing at a hotel (and I won't call the name) and somebody came up to us and they asked us to play the 'Big Bamboo'. He knows that 'Big Bamboo' is not a song that you can play when there are a lot of children around. So we had to tell them no, we cannot play that song. The response went down well, as we explained that it was a children's resort. We even ran a joke to get them to further understand.

The experiences Palmer gained from being a member and owner of bands influenced his development as an individual. He sees where they have made him calmer and more helpful to other persons:

You might have some people who really love music – like one member in my band who really loves music but music didn't love him. If you hear him now it is a different thing, because all I said to him was that he needed to practise, practise, and practise. That person has really done well and I have seen where I have helped him.

Palmer argues that despite being the only visually impaired person in the band, at times sighted persons take their sight for granted and this can be detrimental in music. "Music is all listening and hearing. Because if something is wrong in your ears, you a go get a little setback there. So I think the sighted people who I am working with, they take their sight for granted most of the time."

Nevertheless, he cannot remember an incident where he faced discrimination because of his visual impairment. This he attributes to his practice of informing people of his disability soon after meeting them, which leads to them protecting him. Though he says the treatment he receives is similar to that which a sighted person would get, and he would not have it any other way. On the subject of his longevity in the field, he attributes this to the many hours of hard work, rehearsal, and the dedication the band has displayed over the years:

Rehearsal has ensured longevity. Sometimes you don't know that some songs may be important five years down the line. A tourist may come up to you and say, 'Could you play 'Moon Walk'?' Or 'Could you play... (some way out song)?' As a band, you have to rehearse and you have to stay together. Because the moment somebody cracks, that's the moment the band cracks. We don't do much road work... outside of the hotel. The most of our jobs are on the inside. So say, for example, we are going to do a 'Jamaica night' performance, we have to do Jamaican songs. You have to get back to your roots where you have to play Miss Lou songs; 'Banana Boat' songs. You have to know them.

With all that Palmer has accomplished, his motivation to improve is as strong as ever. He says the biggest challenge faced by the bands is the infrequency with which they work – especially the reggae band. Such a situation impacts on their income and the ability to secure certain necessities, such as a vehicle to transport the bands:

Sometimes the guys would say, 'Mr Palmer, we need some more work.' That is one of the things I need to work on because getting a reggae band work entails a lot of things – for example, transporta-tion. Without it you won't be able to get by. There are a lot of hotels, and if they call me to work I cannot go because transporta-tion is a lot of money.

The need to accommodate the tourists by performing work from their own culture figures prominently on Palmer's to-do list:

We are going to try next year to see if we can do some research on, say for example, songs from Canada, the United States, and Germany... Once you hear 'One Love', you instantly know that that is a Bob Marley song. So we are going to do research on the popular songs from some [other] countries.

The music industry has changed significantly from that which existed when he initially started out. For example, the songs today are much easier to play and in his opinion there is not much meaning attached to them. In terms of being remembered, he says he does not mind if he went down in history as the band that does not play certain kinds of music, like those songs with gun lyrics. In this regard, he does have one recommendation he hopes the government would one day pass into law:

One day I would like to hear the government say anybody who sings negative music, for example about woman's [body] parts, or bad people, or gun lyrics should be fined around $50 thousand. This is because music is what young people listen to, and if we can't have a hold on the music then our young people a go stray very fast.

Palmer has critical advice to impart:

For a visually impaired person wishing to enter music, you have to learn to play an instrument. Because you can now express yourself. Whenever you have friends and people around who you have to work with, let them know you are visually impaired. Because if you should [come upon] a hole and you don't say anything to them, you are going to fall in that hole.

Though catering to distinct audiences, Peter Clarke and Devon Palmer have stamped their authority on the music industry. They have demonstrated that irrespective of the circumstances that confront an individual in life, with grit and determination, that person can be successful. They have identified that music works for them; they have learnt the art and science of their craft and are making an honest living from their chosen careers. At the same time, they are immensely impacting their audiences while contributing significantly to the cultural advancement of Jamaica.

Frankie Paul:
The "Tu-Sheng Peng" General

I don't smoke cigarettes 'cause it will stop I breath
Yes, yeah
I-man don't sniff coke 'cause it will make I choke
Oh well
Oh well
See!
All I smoke is the real tu-sheng peng
Tu-sheng peng make I count from one to ten
Pass the tu-sheng peng, pass it over
Woii!
So, pass the tu-sheng peng, pass it over
Ohh

(Paul "Frankie Paul" Blake 1984)

One of the most iconic figures in dancehall music in Jamaica, Frankie Paul is amongst the most popular solo artistes with a disability in Jamaican music.

Born Paul Blake, Frankie Paul (October 19, 1965–May 18, 2017) was often referred to as Jamaica's Stevie Wonder. A talented multi-instrumentalist with a tremendous range, also affectionately known as "Dancehall Paul", he was visually impaired, and although in childhood he had surgery on a hospital ship to correct this, only 30 per cent of his sight returned. Frankie was a part of a huge family which included seven sisters and three brothers. His father died when he was very young and his mother, Grace Kerr, a street trader, later married Lloyd Clarke, an electrician.

Despite his obvious impairment, Frankie was determined to forge a career in the music business (*Jamaica Observer* 2017). While attending the Salvation Army School for the Blind and Visually Impaired, he would resort to drastic measures in order to record. Edgar Morgan, a close friend, recalled how he would flirt with danger on a daily basis:

> While at school, I was his eyes and ears per se. Because there was a time when he was doing a stint with High Times (recording with them) and, like, he would leave out early; so he would ask me to make sure the coast was clear because the rule was that you were not to leave without the administration's permission. Being that I was a day student, I got permission and I could go and come as I wished. So he would use me as the scapegoat to get him out on the road. He went, did his recordings and came back; and it just started there.

His peers viewed Paul as a jovial and comical person. He was also seen as one who lived life to the fullest and for a brief period he contemplated whether or not to venture into radio, often pretending to be the announcer behind the microphones.

Morgan said he had a very mischievous side to him which went unnoticed by many students at the time:

> [As] a day student, I would come in with my lunch and Paul would, as the saying goes, 'smell me out'. He would say 'Oooooo! Edgar is here!' He would just feel for my lunch pan and grab it. School started at 8:30 a.m. and I would be missing the pan from 8:30 a.m. until about say 11–11:30 a.m. when we would get lunch [and he returned it] minus a few contents. But what are friends for? I would then in turn have to go back on the road and buy my lunch as between Paul and the others they really went through my lunch pan. Then, he would always call my mother and say, 'Mrs Morgan, you should fix the same lunch for Edgar every day because I like it!'

Morgan recounts that Paul was not your typical student and therefore was not interested in "book and pencil". Instead he was always the first person to be called upon when an event was held at the school to rehearse and entertain the visitors. He was also the master of other instruments such as the piano, the guitar, and the drum. His career got a boost when his idol, world renowned Stevie Wonder, visited the school. In an interview with Angus Taylor in December 2011 which appeared in the online reggae magazine, *United Reggae*, Paul recounted how the day unfolded and how the authorities at the school tried concealing what was being planned:

> Ah! It was a wonderful day. It was raining a little in the morning. The school bell rang but we didn't know what was happening. They told us we were going to have a surprise! We all went to the assembly hall and we saw keyboards set up and a microphone and I was saying, 'Who's this?' and I saw them bringing him on stage. I thought, 'Stevie Wonder, my idol!' And it was fabulous. A wonderful time. I got up on stage and sang 'I Can See Clearly Now' and Stevie Wonder said, 'Oh. Beautiful voice you've got there. Keep it up and I hope you become international with it.' And here I am today. They call me the Jamaican Stevie Wonder.

His first official recording came when he was at the tender age of 15 with a single titled "African Princess". His career blossomed at the turn of the 1980s and his hit-making skills began to bear fruit. After Frankie's death, Earl "Chinna" Smith, his former mentor and producer, in an interview on CVM's OnStage in 2017, spoke of the first time he heard and saw him. He said he remembered it as if it were yesterday:

> *We have this record company High Times Records, and some bredrin I think from Trench Town bring this artiste downtown; but the unique thing bout him is like him wi just start sing and a crowd of people just appear. And you would watch this yute ya; everywhere him go is like him sing like every song. For example, he could sing the top 10 and do it the same way like the original. So my bredrin Missa Brown, who was a part of the High Times Records say, 'We go record this bredrin enu.' So we carry him to Tuff Gong and record his first song. At the time we were releasing Muta album, Check It, so we dress him up and buy him suit and Frankie just mash up the place.*

He quickly rose to such prominence that he upstaged another of his idols, Beres Hammond, in England. Speaking on the same CVM programme, Copeland Forbes, Paul's former personal manager recounted:

> *He was fresh on the scene and this was the first time I saw the line around the Brixton Academy go around about four times or five times; and this was the coming of this new prince who was talented. Him have the voice, he can imitate, and he was the greatest*

deliverer. And believe you me when this youth come on the scene, well dress in his suit and with his signature sound 'Awwwwww!' the place turn over. Ironically, he was even introduced by Dennis Brown himself who, despite living in England, came home and made several appearances with Frankie at events – notably Sunsplash.

His confidence, with the knowledge that he could hold his own alongside the stalwarts of his generation, led to a series of hits which reverberated beyond Jamaica's shores. It started with a Channel One Showtime series featuring him across two volumes. One featured him with Sugar Minott and the other included Little John. Songs included "Worries in the Dance", "Pass the Tu-Sheng Peng", "Tidal Wave", "Alesha", "Casanova", "Sara", "Fire Deh a Mus Mus Tail", "Slow Down", and many others.

"Pass the Tu-Sheng Peng" and "Worries in the Dance" are arguably two of his most popular songs. Paul revealed that they both were inspired by the environment in which he found himself on two separate occasions. In his previously mentioned December 2011 interview with Angus Taylor, he chronicled:

'Worries in the Dance'... I was in the dance one time and the girls were acting real outrageous – dancing on their head and they were going down on the floor, and I was saying, 'This look like worries man!' So immediately I went to Channel One and I did the first version for this guy George [Phang] that came from Canada. 'Tu-Sheng Peng'... I was coming from a cabaret show in Negril and my friend said, 'Wh'appen? We go have a Tu-Sheng Peng in the house'; and my other friend said, 'Tu-Sheng Peng does the man nough.' I thought, 'Wha? Them got me now call Tu-Sheng Peng?' So I just asked them if I could use it. They said yes, and I sang 'Pass the Tu-Sheng Peng, Pass It Over.'

Junjo Lawes, one of Paul's former producers, was one of the most feared persons in the 1980s, and people were afraid of associating themselves with him. Continuing his *United Reggae* December 2011 interview, Paul said:

At first I was scared of him because I had heard he was a bad man and he used to tie up people and do all kind of things. So I said to myself, 'I am going to see who is Junjo?' So when they locked the studio I was in there hiding, because no one was allowed in there when Junjo was recording. So I went into the studio and he said, 'Who this little boy I-yah?' And I said, 'I can sing you know'; and he said, 'Let me hear you.' So he put on a rhythm, I sang, and the whole place went berserk! He was like, 'Yo! Give him five more riddim!' and they gave me five more rhythms and I sang. When I had finished recording he had one of those brown paper bags filled with money and said, 'This is yours.' I went home and me and my friends sat down counting out pure twenty dollars – at the time no hundred dollar [bills] were [in circulation] in Jamaica; it was just twenty dollars. We counted, counted, counted, and we got a lot of money at the time – which was nice! It was nice working with Junjo because he was a man that paid! He treated the artistes good.

A tug-of-war ensued between companies over signing him to their labels. They all recognized his worth and knew his potential value. Chinna Smith, who was working with him at the time, experienced this first hand:

> Jammy's brother came in and move him although we did have him under contract; [we] never have any money so we couldn't sue him. But because he was so talented we knew great things would happen to him. He was under my mentorship for around two years and he was like a star in the ghetto.

Despite leaving, Paul was forever grateful for what Chinna did for his career, and noted that getting the break with his first track, laid the foundation for all he had achieved.

His versatility stood out and his innovativeness was there for all to see. Morgan, who knew him better than many, said he could do his own promos, and "you could give Paul a tin can and Paul could make magic with it." Chinna concurred, "You could just take any rhythm and play and him could sing any tune on it. It could even sound like the rhythm make for that song. Hence he was given the name Dancehall Paul."

For Forbes, who began managing him in the 1990s, his voice range and ability to hold notes were just out of this world:

> This all started when I started a tour called 'Reggae Superfest'. That started out with Dennis Brown, Freddy McGregor, and Stitchie; and when it broke down I had Dennis Brown, Beres

Hammond, Andrew Tosh, and Frankie Paul. That was when I really saw his talent. That guy was so talented he played around ten instruments. In Japan 2002 it was unbelievable. He had the greatest baritone pitch. He could go any range. I have a gospel album at home that never release and he played every instrument on it. Drums, keyboards, everything.

Entertainment consultant and radio DJ Michael Barnett, who promoted four Startime concerts that featured Paul, chose to work with him because of his easy-going personality and his huge catalogue which made him stand out from many other artistes in his generation: "Frankie was an exceptional artiste and superstar of the 80s/90s with an amazing voice and range. He was always able to please any audience with his large catalogue of hits to choose from." Barnett said it was important to show him that you cared about his well-being and that he could trust that you had his best interests at heart.

Paul performed over 5,000 songs but was never affected by the paradigm shift which swept the music industry with the introduction of digital music. He still preferred live music, about which he said:

It gives you more deeper inner feeling. It makes you think of original things. Original things happening around you. It's not like camouflage. The digital thing is camouflage. But you know, you can still make the digital thing sound like it's live. If you put your heart and your mind to it, it will sound live.

He stressed the importance of artistes looking after their voices throughout their careers, and his own voice remained in tip-top shape over the years. But how was he able to manage this? He explained:

Well… I do a lot of practice, testing it out every day. Make sure it's working properly. Make sure all the notes are there. All the slurs are there. The energy's there. And the vibes is there. So there is nothing I leave out. And the prayer. Most important thing of all is the prayer. I do a prayer before I do anything in this world today so God can look upon his son and give me more blessings.

He believed Jamaica's music was in good health despite the changes the industry had undergone. He pointed to the explicit nature of the music and the level of violence attributed to it. He much preferred the "old stuff" as what was on offer did not appeal to him. He also believed that there were a whole lot of good artistes around but they were not fully maximizing their potential:

They are scared to get out there and do their thing due to what's happening now. What we have to do now is get back to the roots and remember that it's God, the Most High God, nothing else, nobody else that runs the thing. He probably is not too quick at doing what some people want him to do but it surely will come someday.

Apart from his music, he had an infectious personality which seemed to radiate to anyone in his vicinity. He valued friendship above all and would go above and beyond the call of duty for those he respected. This trait, according to Morgan, also made him special and a good friend to have:

After leaving school, we lost touch for a while. Then I heard there was a stage show at Cinema 2 and I did not tell him I was coming. I was outside waiting to get in and he came by and heard me talking to some other people and said, 'Ooooo, Edgar deya!' And I was back stage for the entire performance living like a king. After that we just exchanged house numbers as at the time cell phones were not so popular and we just kept in touch. I had all his numbers – Gambia, U.S. (New York), and England. So, I could find him at a moment's notice.

Once he separated himself from one of his backroom staff as that person had disrespected Morgan who was also visually impaired.

I remember we were at one of the hotels and one of the guys said something about me that he did not like. He got really upset and tore that guy from limb to limb. As a result of that, that person left his company. I don't know if that person expected him to take up for him, but Paul was having none of it. We just had each other's backs.

Morgan revealed that he (Paul) was a spur-of-the-moment person and that added to his unpredictability:

Strange enough, Paul did me something that I will never forget. He came to the house the Monday and said to me, 'Edgar, come with me. We going to the country.' I told my parents I going country with Paul. Let's say that was Monday January 1ˢᵗ. You know when I came back? January 22. This was just with the clothes on my back. He was just a spur-of-the-moment person. He goes out for a day, just know that it is not a day alone. You might be there for a month with Paul. But, you are well taken care of; especially me. I don't know what it was but I guess it was because we were such good friends. I was always looked after by Paul. Everybody else would fend for themselves but Edgar was well taken care of.

For Barnett, some of his major strengths were his memory, his booming voice, his spiritual strength despite his visual challenges, his mastery of the stage and his humility. Paul left an indelible mark on him which has served as great motivation. He notes, "I have learned that no matter your condition or situation, you can become a success in life if you have ambition, self-motivation and determination." He has been in the music industry for over 30 years, and believes other artistes who are facing tribulations should look at Paul's journey and use it as inspiration for what can be achieved: "No matter what your disability or shortcoming may be, you can become the best at your craft, as long as you focus and work towards your goal." He believes Frankie Paul will be remembered as a breath of fresh air in a polluted world. Also, that history will ultimately see him as a great Jamaican singer, and an amazing role model for persons with disabilities.

Morgan says Paul served as a great inspiration to him when experiencing some of his darkest days:

I was [feeling] down when I realize I had a sight problem, but seeing Paul go through his I said, why am I fussing/worrying? I can still move up and down, still have my speech, still have my legs to move up and down and I just looked at it and say if Paul can be that jovial with his disability, why not me? So I just put it aside and I worked with it.

He believed Paul was the master of masking disappointments without anybody recognizing it: "Paul did not make disappointments worry him. He was always upbeat. Yes, he said he prayed but I did not see a downside to him. He just had a good way of mastering his disability. He worked with it well and he just was there for everybody."

In the latter years of his life Paul suffered from kidney problems along with other complications. Because of this, he had to undergo expensive dialysis treatment, which left him in financial difficulties (*Jamaica Gleaner* 2017b). He had lost a leg to diabetes in 2016

(*Jamaica Observer* 2016) and lost his battle with illness at The University Hospital of the West Indies in St Andrew on May 18, 2017 (*Jamaica Gleaner* 2017c). He was 51.

In paying tribute, Minister the Honourable Olivia Grange spoke highly of his involvement in Jamaica's music:

> *He has contributed significantly to our musical heritage. I daresay Frankie Paul (who was visually impaired but not totally blind) should be grouped with the likes of Stevie Wonder and Ray Charles. He has gone from us in the flesh, but the music of Paul Blake will forever live in our hearts.*

Opposition spokesperson on entertainment Natalie Neita-Headley only had glowing words to describe the impact that Paul had made:

> *Frankie Paul never wavered and had one of the nicest voices of his generation – the early dancehall generation – creating memorable hits like 'Worries in the Dance', 'Tidal Wave', 'Pass the Tu-Sheng Peng', 'Cassanova', and 'Sara'. His unique voice, rough and gravelly but with strength, power and range, thrilled us all. Jamaica has lost another pioneer in Frankie Paul and we are all the worse for that loss.*

Despite all Paul achieved, his close friend Morgan still believes there was a lot left in the tank:

> *If he got the backing of management and family he could have gone a far way. Even with his illness, if he got the support, he could have been looked after and right now he would have been here with us. Because I heard there was an interview with the English set where they were doing the procedure for his leg. They got it [the prosthesis], but he said he wanted to come out here, but I don't know if it was to get little sun; and unfortunately he did not go back over. The legs were gotten, proceeds were made so I don't know. But he was gone too soon. Paul had a lot more to give.*

The indefatigable Paul "Frankie Paul" Blake might have died at age 51 but he left an inestimable mark on Jamaican music. Singing and recording over five thousand songs is an extraordinary feat. It is even more so because it was done by a person with a visual disability who never allowed it to impede his contribution to Jamaica's advancement. By his example, he unequivocally promoted persons with disabilities, as his musical works proved him to have had a major impact on Jamaica's culture. The community of persons with disabilities and the broader Jamaican society owe a debt of gratitude to him for his stellar contribution. Indeed, Frankie Paul was a colossus in the music and entertainment industry of Jamaica.

10

The Selectors:
DJ Vision and DJ Ray

Dwayne "DJ Vision" Hamilton

The bread basket parish of St Elizabeth is famous not only for its production of amazing ground provisions but also for its production of Duwane "DJ Vision" Hamilton. This astute and professional selector can justifiably claim the title of veteran selector in the Jamaican dancehall as he has been satisfying its disciples for well over two decades. He assumed the name "DJ Vision" as, though he lacks physical sight, he believes he possesses the foresight, vision and the versatility to entertain. DJ Vision started as one of those home-based entertainers who played music for his friends and neighbours, who were often impressed by his ability.

A blind teacher by the name of Mr Coombs (now deceased) lived on Mannings Hill Road and had a sound system called "Love Ingredients". While Dwayne was at the Salvation Army School for the Blind and Visually Impaired, he would purchase records, and it was convenient for him to take them to Mr Coombs and practice playing on his sound system. This is how he pushed himself into the industry: "In 1992 mi use to buy two records and go ova a man name Mr Coombs and play on his sound... Mi did like music. It jus did fun an di whole engineering part of it. An fi a man weh naa si, yuh zi mi."

Music was his love and his reality, and inspired his functioning as a selector. He himself was dumbfounded by his ability to actually manipulate the audio equipment. He mastered this and pushed forward along this path fully dedicated to his craft, and by 1995, after honing his skills in the industry, he started his own sound system called Supa Mix.

DJ Vision started with a small system that consisted of two bass boxes, two top-end speakers and a rack of tweeters. His older brother who had earlier migrated to the United States, assisted him with the funds to acquire two additional large size speaker boxes. His sound system began its transition!

Though this was for him a dream come true, his lack of sight was a challenge. Back then, DJs had to use vinyl and as this only allowed for the taping of one track, the DJ was compelled to walk with a large collection of records to serve for the duration of the dance. This proved problematic for DJ Vision as, being blind, he knew there would be a difficulty deciphering the different records. He was afraid of playing the "wrong" song at the "wrong" time. But he quickly discovered a strategy for circumventing this issue. He would employ a file keeper who would be in control of the vinyl records and hand him the needed record upon request: "It did sticky fi mi when picking out di records dem tru dem neva have on Braille. But mi use one youth weh always roun mi and tell him seh him in charge a di records, so whenever mi need a different one mi jus tell him and him look fi it fi mi."

From the Turntable to the Laptop

The early 2000s presaged the era of CDs for many disc jockeys and sound system operators. While there were a few who were not willing to make the switch, many took advantage of the advent of this new technology. For DJ Vision it meant even more autonomy. As a consequence, he was able to dispense with the intermediary and quickly move from vinyl to CD and from Discman to CD Machine and then onto laptops. He elucidated:

> Yuh si when yuh a use CD yuh can jus put more than one song on it and that mean seh yuh naa go use wul epp a [a whole heap of] CD like when yuh a use a lot a records. Suh yuh know seh when yuh a use CD yuh put what yuh want on one CD and what yuh want on a next CD. And then again now di case dem can tek the braille, so mi able to find the CD that I want [by myself]. As the technology move mi work wid it man. Same way mi move on from Discman and use CD Machine and now mi have a laptop. Mi neva figure out dem same time, but mi tek time feel dem out and after dat dem nuh give mi nuh trouble.

Unbelievable Talent

Clayton Hilton, who is a sound system operator himself, has worked with DJ Vision since 1995. In an interview with this researcher,

Hilton, known as "DJ Sweely", said he and other dancehall fans were incredulous when they witnessed DJ Vision in action: "He's just unbelievable, the way how he party with the crowd." Sweely assists DJ Vision in the dancehall, and attests to the fact that people are just in awe when watching this gentleman in full flight: "At first everyone was stunned. They stared all night." When asked if he felt that DJ Vision met expectations as a selector, he remarked, "Each party we played, people road block. Everyone came to see a blind man playing sound."

In retrospect, DJ Vision is grateful for his many achievements in the industry and the growth of his sound system. He acknowledged that the use of his laptop assisted him tremendously in helping him to manipulate the system and significantly aided the quality of his output. He however admits that it also poses its own challenges in the form of what he describes as "traffic". A lot more persons are joining the market because of the ease of accessibility that the laptop now affords the user. According to him, he and many other DJs are currently facing downtime in the business because of the fierce competition.

Nevertheless, he would encourage all aspiring DJs with a disability to feel free to come aboard. He says he has lived it and learned that people will appreciate you as long as you possess the talent. Because of his own talent he has managed to overcome the perceptions of the sceptics who were at first surprised to learn of his disability. He reminisces about the days when DJs were allowed to play music from early in the evening straight back into the wee hours of the following morning. But he also longs to hear more well put together lyrics as was the standard during his former years, and he yearns for the return of the days of clean and wholesome lyrics which promoted proper values and attitudes.

Rayon "DJ Ray" Campbell: Saved by the Music

Rayon Campbell, "DJ Ray", attended the Salvation Army School for the Blind and Visually Impaired until 1997, after which he graduated to Jamaica College, located at Old Hope Road in St Andrew. He stayed there for five years before moving to England in 2002. There he works as a disc jockey and radio presenter, and continues to contribute to the internationalization of Jamaica's music. Though he is totally blind he has managed to lift himself beyond his misfortune into a world where he began to see himself as someone with abilities, rather than focusing on his disability.

Living in the United Kingdom and working as a DJ can be very challenging at times, especially for one just entering the market as it is very competitive. Clients are looking to ensure they are hiring someone who is able to multitask while entertaining the crowd. They are in search of someone who is able to play the "right" music at the "right" time and at the right place. They are also in search of someone who is able to provide entertainment through speech while playing music. But most of all, they need someone who has a large enough fan base to complement and heighten the vibe of the event – that is, someone who is popular.

DJ Ray explained what his entrance into the music business meant to him. In the latter part of 2008 he says he experienced a season of total darkness. He was battling personal problems, struggling to press through them. During his fight for survival, he found himself in a mental asylum where the only thing that kept him sane was listening to instrumental music, as his turmoil forced him to isolate himself from the voices of other people:

> I started doing DJ at what I would consider one of the darkest times in my life. I was going through a lot of personal things, a lot of struggles and the one thing that was bearable for me was music. I could not listen to books; I couldn't listen to the radio if people were gonna talk on it. I just couldn't listen to anybody else's voice. I just needed the music.

During this exile he educated himself on how to mix CDs, and to his surprise, not only was he able to stop buying them, but even better, by 2009 he could sell his own, having understood how to use the software. For DJ Ray this was life-saving. Encouraged by his accomplishments, in 2010 he created his Facebook page and began to send out posts advertising himself as a disc jockey:

> I remember starting to research how to do my mixes and to see if that would be possible. And when I started to do my mixes and I started to sell my mix CDs (this is January 2009), and I realized the more I went ahead doing this, the more I started to love it. I figured that I don't even need to go out to Brixton Market and buy mix CDs anymore! I can do this! I can do this myself!
>
> By 2010 I thought I had to create my Facebook. So, I read it through and verify that I am in on the market if anyone is looking for DJs; and I have been doing [it] ever since.

It was not long before it dawned on him that it took more than just his ability to play music for him to flourish in the sound system business. He realized he needed to have a certain image, as that is what persons initially saw, and from which they created their own idea of the type of DJ he might be. He says:

> As a blind DJ you face added problems – cosmetics and presumption. Some people may be happy with the music you play but they are going for some kind of flashy look as a part of their package and for some reason they think you don't fit that image. 'You're disabled, you're blind, walking with your cane.' And that's an awkward moment.

He tells of having experienced situations where he was chosen above other contestants when playing for audiences who could not see them. However, when clients saw he was blind, they began to question his ability to do the job, even though they had just experienced his skill. In such instances he had had to start over and audition as an individual whom they had never before heard playing music. "I have been in a couple of situations where I have played down my sight just to get the job and when I got the job I found that they were behaving awkward," he relates. "And then you have to do a lot of talking, you have to talk them down, you have to silence them, and convince them that you can do the job."

Sometimes people do view persons with a disability as being the odd ones out; as ones that do not belong; and as ones that cannot complete any task without flaws. Selector Ray bemoans this reality: "Presumptions are a different thing. They will just not let go of the belief that a blind person will just not do it; just will not cut it."

When Selector Ray was asked how he really pulled through with the challenges of not having a large fan base, he explained that this was one of his major obstacles, as people knew he was not into clubbing. Nevertheless, this did not entirely stifle his business:

> The club scene is all about trend, it's all about looks. If you can gather enough people [who] like your personality [and] presentation and you can bring them with you to the club you are playing, then you have a chance. It's a popular thing now for DJs to be asked if they have a fan base already. So competing with that is very tough. And most of the people I know are on Facebook and they don't want to go out to the club; they hardly like it. And being a DJ its tough getting work – but I have managed it.

DJ Ray has played at numerous venues in the United Kingdom with the largest crowd being at the South Bank – a university and arts complex on the southern bank of the Thames River in London – both in 2011 and 2012. He also played for another famous event in King's Cross, London, and at house parties, weddings, birthday parties and charity events. In encouraging other upcoming blind DJs, he advises that when presenting at any event where the client is not known personally, it is best to approach the venue with nerves made of steel. He has found that most people are not accustomed to being open-minded while there are some who definitely choose to be close-minded. Therefore, he warns that they will judge your ability to do the job. He further advises how, as a blind DJ, the clues of honest reaction may be identified in a crowd:

> *If they are generally honest then it's frustration. If they are very patronizing then its pity. 'Oh he's probably having problems and needs some help.' Personally, I prefer the honest reaction. But it does happen. Try to make a name for yourself in a market where there are literally hundreds of people going for the one job. It's tough, but you always have to be at your best. You always have to be ready to take the knocks when they come and be ready to go for long periods.*

Over the years Ray's love for music has turned into a passion, and despite the odds it is still his desire to continue doing it. He hopes that one day he will be a resident DJ, chosen to play regularly at a specific event as often it is held; so he is working on his image and his music quality. Since December 2014 he has been a DJ presenter on an online radio station called Dodge Radio in the United Kingdom. At this point in his career he is pleased with his growth, having moved from mixing CDs to operating as a DJ to now having three shows on the station: "I do three shows, Sunday Souls at 7:00 p.m., Reggae Explosion at 10:00 p.m. on a Tuesday, and Saturday Night Party at 7:00 p.m. on a Saturday." He has also been able to expand his fan base to the European market, having listened to them, and adjusted his image as he got a deeper understanding of what they liked.

DJ Vision and DJ Ray have claimed their space in the dancehall, the clubs, and on the airwaves. They have done so with distinction and contributed to the advancement of Jamaica's culture. Without a doubt, they have demonstrated that wherever they are given the opportunity to participate, they will do so with excellence. They make a compelling case for greater inclusion of persons with disabilities in all aspects of society.

11

Fabulous Five: The Jewel in the Crown of Jamaica's Roots Rocking Reggae Music

Every woman deserve a good buddy,
every woman should have a good buddy
Every woman deserve a good buddy,
every woman should have a good buddy
I know some very lonely women,
who have good jobs and lots of money to spend
Some a dem don't even have no children
and worse of all dem say dem tired a men
So hear we me ask dem: wa man du yu
Dem get too up tight and every likkle ting dem want fus and fight
Dem husband don't not at all,
dem get too jealous when you get phone call
Sugar daddy? No him wont do
Him pocket full up a money but him can't
Su way u want
A boy friend
What you want
A real good friend
What you want
A real good man friend
Ooooooooooooooooooooo!
You need a buddy   (Fab Five 1995)

Fab Five is undoubtedly the most successful musical band in Jamaica. One of the country's most sought-after reggae/soca bands, they have lasted over 50 years and produced a plethora of songs that have become chart-busters locally, regionally and internationally.

This dynamic group has also captivated diverse audiences with their vocals, dynamism, charm and creativity. Others have tried to emulate them but are seen as mere imitators.

Fab Five originated in the Bronco Night Club in Union Square in Cross Roads, St Andrew in 1968. As manager and band leader Frankie Campbell recalled in an interview with the *Jamaica Gleaner* on the occasion of their 40th anniversary, there was no inclination to continue long-term:

> When we started 40 years ago, we started to get girls and popularity. We never thought that we would be around for 40 years. As young people, we loved music, but in the early days we played for the fun of it, never from a business side. We learned after a while that it is a business, and we have to live off it (*Jamaica Gleaner* 2010).

Brothers Conroy and Grub Cooper who are both visually impaired and past students of the Salvation Army School for the Blind and Visually Impaired as well as Frankie Campbell who was just out of Kingston College were the pioneers. As would become apparent, all of them sang on their respective choirs while attending school. At the start, Conroy was the keyboard player, Grub was the drummer, and Frankie played bass. For it to be successful, they sought the services of a few others whose primary roles were to sing. They got their first job as a hotel band in 1969, and incorporated guitar player Junior Bailey.

Their original name could no longer be used, as it was based on the name of the establishment where they had worked previously. Their new owners decided to call them the Fabulous Five which was then shortened to Fab Five. In 1970 they decided to expand, and Steve Golding and Peter Scarlet joined. They transitioned from playing in hotels to becoming a road band as there was now more impetus to travel and perform. According to Frankie Campbell, this was very important in their early development:

> *In other words, we came out of the hotel circuit or the night club circuit as the resident band, [playing] four, five, or six nights a week [and we became instead] a road band, meaning that we played at various functions all over the island, as people wanted us. That's what a road band does. Therefore, we hit the road in 1970 November – with me Frankie Campbell on bass; Grub Cooper, drums/vocals; Conroy Cooper, keyboard/vocals; Steve*

Golding, guitar/vocals; Junior Bailey, guitar/vocals; and Peter Scarlett, lead vocals – as a six-piece aggregation.

Still they stuck with the name, and in its embryonic stages, Fab Five's work began to gain recognition with a string of works and awards.

One of the turning points came when they did Johnny Nash's album *I Can See Clearly Now* in 1971. It was critical, because even though they were not being paid, being a very young band the members were excited to play for such an international icon who had received several awards. The only recognition they wanted was the credits for the album. According to Campbell, this was strategic as they realized that all the songs on the album would be hits which would become popular. Also, it would speak volumes for them going forward if it was made known that they were associated with a person of such high esteem. However, as fate would have it, no credit or recognition was given.

According to Campbell, this was a difficult pill to swallow considering the amount of work and time that went into the project. He however comforted himself that it was all a learning experience and it would make them stronger individuals. "It was hard, as we would be touring in America and watching television and seeing them announcing a song from the album being at number one, and knowing we were the ones behind it."

Their first recording, "Come Back and Stay", was number one in Jamaica, and in their first year on the road and for the following two years, they won the only available local awards – the Swing Awards for Best Band of 1971–72, 1972–73 and 1973–74. They also shared the El Suzie Award for Top Road and Dance Band for 1975–76 with another band, and won the RJR Listeners' Award for Best Band in 1980.

They expanded throughout the 1970s despite being forced to constantly re-invent themselves with the frequent changes in the industry. Sidney Thorpe, who is totally blind, joined the band in 1979 and benefited from these changes. He says:

When Conroy Cooper left in 1979, that laid the door open for me to come in as keyboard player. So I left straight out of school [and went] into Fab Five as a holiday job. Since I didn't go to study again (because I was supposed to go away to Canada to study), Fab Five took me on permanently.

In order to remain relevant in what was a very competitive music environment, the band had to invent ways to further market itself. Thorpe recalled that when they decided to enter the soca arena this was far from straightforward:

A number of years later on, of course, the dynamics of the band changed. Then, with the advent of soca, we brought in horns. Fab Five had recorded a song called 'You Safe' in 1985 and in order to perform it on stage we needed horns. So, we brought in horns because by then, 1986, we had recorded a soca album which was the first original soca album out of Jamaica, and on it we had a lot of songs that required horn players. So we brought in two horns and ended up having seven people (because we didn't have a vocalist out front anymore).

This subtle change proved an instant success as it led to a large catalogue of soca hits that not only proved popular to Jamaicans but to people all across the Caribbean. Songs such as "You Safe", "Ring Road Jam", "Feeling Horny", "Jamaican Woman", "All Night Party", "Mini", "Sweat", "Good Buddy", and "Mango" were just a few tracks which had people in a frenzy whenever they were played.

Recognition, according to Frankie Campbell, was not as difficult as he thought it would be. Due to the groundwork done by them in their first year and their first award, life became much easier. Their uniqueness as well as their youthful exuberance and showmanship further increased their popularity. They had fans from all walks of life eating out of the palms of their hands where music was concerned. "In those days, it took us about three months and we were touring," he recalls.

We were launched in November 1970, and by January 1971 we went to Cayman with Winston Blake and Merritone, who was a big producer at the time. By that year we were touring because we made such a big impact. In those days, there wasn't social media. In those days, you had one TV station. You came on TV once, then you made an impact, then you made your name, and that's what we did. By '71 we had our first hit record, 'Come Back and Stay', produced by Harry J. Therefore, we made our name very easily, but because of hard work and talent, you know. In other words, a lot of bands were there [and] could make their name like Fab Five, but we made a big impact very quickly. By the end of the decade we were a household name, doing all the major shows [including]

CARIFESTA [a regional festival of arts and culture hosted by a different Caribbean country on each occasion].

This recognition saw the band working and rubbing shoulders with some of the best and most popular personalities in the music industry from Jamaica and around the world. Individuals and groups like Jimmy Cliff, Bob Marley, Roy Rayon, Sean Paul, Ray Charles, Dizzy Gillespie, the Grateful Dead, Roberta Flack, Fats Domino, the ChiLites, the Drifters, the Mighty Sparrow, Aretha Franklin, Gladys Knight, the Manhattans, the Delphonics, Shaggy, Joe Jackson, Peter Tosh, Grace Thrillers, Gem Myers, and Eric Donaldson are just a few who have benefited from their services. Major collaborations have been done with the likes of Marcia Griffiths, Beres Hammond, Queen Ifrica, and Richie Stephens. They also backed Johnny Nash on all the reggae cuts comprising most of his platinum album, *I Can See Clearly Now.*

They have also made appearances at several world events. One such event was the anti-nuclear concert in New York's Central Park where there were approximately 1.5 million people in attendance. This story Sidney Thorpe was all too eager to tell:

> *They had a nuclear disarmament rally, and all the bigwigs in rock music and pop music and so on were at the rally. We were backing Rita Marley at the time, and they pulled the plug on some of those people so that Rita Marley could perform. Because, of course, Bob Marley just died, so the name 'Marley' was very big in the minds of the members of the music fraternity... We were at the nuclear disarmament rally and there were a million people in Central Park, New York, and there were another five hundred thousand around the periphery I understand. So, when you hear that applause man, memba mi tell yuh... you ain't heard nothing like that. I mean it was like wow!*

Discipline and dedication are two of the superlatives used by multiple festival song winner Roy Rayon to describe the band. The "Love Fever", "Give Thanks and Praises", "Come Rock" artiste incidentally had all his winning national festival entries produced by the band. Working alongside them from 1980, he said they were always present for both rehearsals as well as for events. During our chat, Sidney (the storyteller) recounted an incident when they had to resort to drastic measures in order to be present at an event:

There was one occasion where Fab Five rented a private jet to come back to Jamaica to perform at a function. What happened was that we had missed our flight and we were in New Orleans. We missed the flight from New Orleans to Miami, so we asked the pilot of Air Jamaica to hold the plane for us so that we could catch up and board the flight in Miami to meet our appointment in Montego Bay. We were supposed to play for Westwood Girls, their 100th Anniversary or something like that. And... well, the plane couldn't hold it no more. So, the plane left, and when we reached Miami, the plane was on the runway getting ready to take off. So you know seh we just would not have caught that plane.

And then, we were in the Miami airport and we said, 'Well, the only other thing to fulfil that engagement [is] to rent a plane.' So we rented a Lear jet from Miami to Montego Bay. When the pilot bundled us into his car, all a we, to take to the airport in Fort Lauderdale where the Lear was waiting, police stop him, and he had to explain to the officer seh, I mean you know, 'I'll deal with you when I come back, because I'm flying out now to take these guys to a gig in Jamaica.' Well, the police were very nice and kind and cooperative, and they said, 'Okay fine.' So him fly we go a Jamaica, at 41,000 feet, with all champagne on board and all those things on the plane. And, we got to Montego Bay, and him just go through customs, turn back round and fly back to Miami, or to Fort Lauderdale, or to wherever the police they want him.

Other events they have graced with their presence include Portia Simpson Miller's farewell function hosted by Prime Minister Andrew Holness at Vale Royal, the St Jude's Anglican Church Harvest Supper, and the Portland Jerk Festival.

With this level of dedication, it is clear to see why there are always new and old clients queuing up for their services. Roy Rayon noted:

What make them so special is how they play the music and deliver it. They are an impressive set of musicians and chemistry is a hell of a thing. There is just a connection there; you can just see it. Apart from the musicians, [there is] the way how they try to encourage you to hone your craft and to do it with discipline.

Their inventiveness led to them putting out a series of CDs on which they covered various songs and sounded just like the original artistes. "We started the live series in 1999," said Frankie Campbell. He remembered:

We did around four additional CDs [before] we decided to abandon the process. We however decided to give it another go to commemorate the Jamaica 50 celebrations. While playing one of these discs in the studio once, a popular artiste who will remain nameless came up to us and was in amazement. He was like, 'Hold on de! How you get all of those guys fi perform fi you?' When his song came, him se, 'Hold on! But me nu memba recording dis? A who dis Grub?' He was really amazed that all the voices he was hearing were not the original people.

He sees music functioning in the same way as a photograph, and as such nothing else compares. According to him, five to ten years can pass without someone hearing a song, yet as soon as it is played one instantly is drawn back to all that had transpired in the period of the song; one instantly remembers everything in the past.

It evokes some emotions in you that are unbelievable. That is what we try to do whenever we go to sessions in New York, Canada or anywhere for that matter. People attend shows to hear, sometimes, music that they have not heard for many years. They want to hear the original stuff and that is what we strive to give our audience, claims Campbell.

At any event at which the band is the main act, people dance and sing with abandon, and just have a good time. Campbell continues:

The crowd has been excellent. Locally, people love Fab Five. They equate Fab Five... like I said, once you mention a band, they think of Fab Five. In Jamaica, once you mention cigarettes, you talk about Craven-A; once you mention beer, you talk about Red Stripe. It's the same with Fab Five. Once you mention band, them think of Fab Five. Our performances are rated and are ranked highly. People enjoy themselves, and that's why we still getting work.

The response and love shown by patrons all over are also due to their good work ethic. According to Sidney Thorpe, these experiences have been critical to the band's development:

Well, the band realized that it is important to have good credit rating. If people don't figure your credit rating is good, them not going to ask you to do things, or employ you to do things. We have a good credit rating when it comes to being on time, when it comes to fulfilling our engagements, when it comes to representing Jamaica, because we have done that so many times.

Like when we go Cuba, for example, we were representing Jamaica at that time. That time, people hardly went to Cuba, because of the political climate in the '70s and early '80s. So, when we went, that was my first engagement with the band in 1979. We went to Cuba for CARIFESTA, and we were guests of the Cuban government.

As a matter of fact, we met Fidel Castro, and shake him hand, and him seh, 'Well, Fab Five must come live a Cuba,' cause well, you get everything free in Cuba. Of course, Castro done know seh we can't come do dat; because we have lots of work in Jamaica as well, and Jamaica people probably would never forgive us. Even though we were number one in Cuba at the time – big, big, big and bigger than anybody else. It has made us understand how important we are, and that the band is bigger than all of us in deh.

Because, Fab Five is a household name, Fab Five is a big family name, we have to make sure that whatever we put out there is family friendly... All kind of those other things; all the variables in between that help with personal development. A lot of us learnt, as blind people how to react to people who don't understand anything about blindness, for example. But, the other thing is that when you are in a group like Fab Five, and you are blind, they don't see a blind person, they see a Fab Five member. So, a guy see me on the road, him seh, 'Fab Five!' Or them would call me by name. Them not going to say, well, 'blindy', 'we yah seh blindaz', [or] whatever they say. I don't know. I'm out of touch with that now; but people usually say that when they don't know your name. But they know my own. So they call me by my name or they might say 'musician!'... whatever.

There are two original members, Grub Cooper – who is blind and plays drums – is the musical director, and Frankie Campbell, who is the manager and one of a few sighted persons in the band. He says he feels honoured to be working alongside persons who have a disability. Actually, he believes this is the most significant reason that the band has achieved so much, as blind people tend to be very focused on whatsoever they are doing:

That's one of the reasons why Fab Five is so successful. Because, by having blind people, people with a disability around us, they are more settled. Blind people don't 'wander like fowl and scatter like peas' like other people outta road. Like all a dem other wayward musicians that look gyal all over the place and carry on. That's why groups don't last very long. Fortunately for us, with us having blind people, they're a little bit more settled. I'm not saying that you don't have blind man who look gyal and ting. All I'm saying is that even if dem a look gyal, dem have to stay on dem base; them available. So, I think that's one of the successes, why we have lasted so long and been so successful, because of that input. Sidney been with us for 30-something years; Donovan, 25 years; Grub, original member; and Mandy been with the organization for 30-something years. He was in Unique Vision from 1978.

Campbell added that the willingness to adjust and adapt to the changing face of the music industry has tremendously helped in their survival:

We are always looking to keep in touch with musical trends. We may not be big fans of today's dancehall music, but every year, there are great songs and we try to make sure that we perform these songs and keep ourselves relevant to the younger generation, maintaining our energy. At the same time we, we periodically infuse new and younger talent into the band so that we maintain our energy and enthusiasm. The other thing is we like what we do and treat it like a job that we are privileged to have, rather than some burden forced on us. Fab Five, with the backing of artistes on shows, and the new songs we put into our bandstand catalogue must be one of the most rehearsed bands in the world. We are constantly in rehearsal.

This is facilitated as band members live within close proximity to each other. At their studio, located in Constant Spring, each member has his own room which is around 10 to 20 seconds walk from the rehearsal base. That means impromptu rehearsal sessions and extra practices are an all too common occurrence.

According to Thorpe: "It's easy to find us for any impromptu situation. Like if a job go come this evening, it easy to find everybody to say, 'Hey, hey! We have a job this evening; or a job tomorrow morning.' We not dispersed all over the world like others, because we're always working." The living arrangement also strengthens the camaraderie between members, which is a critical factor in the band's longevity.

Despite these successes, there are challenges which they face, such as the high cost of maintaining musical equipment necessary for fulfilling engagements and for performing at the level required to satisfy the audience.

Some members with visually impairment also have difficulty writing music as they primarily depend on braille, which can present a challenge with musical notation. As Sidney explains:

I went to the School of Music, and I also did Braille music, but I can't write music like that. I have to... well, I can't write it in Braille either, because Braille music don't set up like that. Anything you have in Braille you have to memorize then practise. We have to memorize a lot of stuff. Like, the first time I went with Fab Five, for that week I had to memorize about 50 tune that I've never played in my life. And also, I had to learn the equipment that I was using, which I never used in my life. So, everything was new. It was one hell of a crash course. Those things help with your development in one way or form.

Sidney who has been blind from birth, believes the music industry is very unforgiving to persons who have a disability. Already disadvantaged due to the lack of sight, he argues that individuals are always fighting people with disabilities, and this means they have to fight twice as hard as their sighted counterparts in order to prove themselves. Even after defying the odds, he reasoned that it serves as the perfect recipe to demotivate them and ultimately may drive them away from fulfilling their dreams. He came up with his own coping mechanisms which he outlines:

I've learned how to be independent. I've learned how to be sure of what I do. I've learned how to stand by whatever decisions I make, because I'm a producer as well. I produce music, and whenever I decide seh a so the music going to go, then I mean is so it going to go. I've learnt a lot about orchestration; how to make things happen the way I want them to, or how to make them happen so that they can be thought to be otherwise. A whole heap of things. I mean, really, it's hard to really encapsulate it.

But despite the challenges, Grub Cooper says that there are no limits to what they can do with music as there would always be more work, be it in touring, recording or film. On their to-do list is the small matter of getting on the Grammy list, arguably the most coveted international accolade that has eluded them thus far. This, according to Sidney would lead to more popularity, more recognition and more work. He also feels that it could lead to them charging people more money for their services. He points out that the publicity that would come with accepting that award on international television could not be paid for. It would not just be about American audiences, but millions of people all over the world would become acquainted with their work.

The band has received 29 local awards between 1986 and 1996 – the most by any music entity in Jamaica's musical history. These were awarded by diverse sources such as JBC, RJR, the *Daily Gleaner*, the *Star*, the Jamaica Music Industry (JAMI), and the Jamaica Federation of Musicians (JFM). They also won the 1995 Rockers Award for Best Band; the 1996 award for Best Group (Instrumental) at the Jamaica Music Awards; a 1999 Tamika Award; the 2000–2002 JFM Best Show Band Award, the Reggae Soca Awards; Best Soca Band 2002–2003; a 2007 Lifetime Achievement Award from Reggae Sumfest; and a 2012 JaRIA Honours Award.

Internationally, honours have included Best Album and Best Single (both won for "Good Buddy") at the Miami Reggae/Soca Awards in 1996; Best International Reggae Album award at the Canadian Reggae Music Awards for *Fab 5 Live – The Ultimate Vintage Jamaican Party Mix. Part 1* in 1999; and also in 1999, Best Soca Album award at the ReggaeSoca Awards in Miami for their album *Shape*, thus making them the first group in history to win best album awards for Reggae and Soca in the same year.

Individual members have also been singled out and recognized locally. Grub Cooper was awarded the Order of Distinction (Officer Class in 1992 and Commander Class in 2006) for his contribution to nation building, and the Musgrave Medal (silver) from the Institute of Jamaica, which puts him in the very elite class of Jamaica's creative artistes. He also got a special honour award in 1988 from the Jamaica Federation of Musicians and, the Rita Marley Foundation honoured him for his contribution to the development of music in 2017. Frankie Campbell has also received the Order of Distinction (Officer Class) in 2000, creating history, as this was the first time a Jamaican musical entity had had two awardees from the same organization. He also received a mentor award from the Jamaica Reggae Industry Association (JaRIA) in 2013.

The band has also been active outside the music industry, for example, working with charitable organizations as well as serving on various boards. In a world where philanthropic activities are becoming as important as work done in the studios and on stage, this shows the versatility of their members, their dedication to nation building, and their willingness to give back to the broader Jamaican society that has supported them over the years. This approach has contributed to their sustainability, to the love of the people which they have so deservedly enjoyed, and in turn will ensure that their place in Jamaicans' hearts will never be questioned.

Fab Five has for over 50 years left a lasting legacy on the Jamaican music industry. Their multiple records, collaborations, collective and individual achievements set them apart from many other bands, and their works have resonated with a wide cross section of the local, regional and international population, which not many bands can boast. Their longevity has surpassed that of many, and their ability to adapt to the changes in the music industry over the years is testament to their discipline, dedication, commitment and hard work, as is their eagerness to educate the next generation of musicians.

As Thomas A. Edison once said, "Genius is 1 percent inspiration and 99 percent perspiration." This adequately sums up the Fabulous Five. Starting out as a hotel band in the late 1960s, they have scaled many heights others have only dreamt of throughout a lifetime.

Love them or hate them, we can all agree that this band has been a true ambassador for Jamaican music and for persons with disabilities, demonstrating that once they get the opportunity to participate and perform, they are going to do so and with excellence. The history of Jamaica's cultural development cannot be written without the inclusion of the contribution of persons with disabilities, and Fab Five is unequivocally qualified to feature in this documentation.

Music has been the tool used by these geniuses who have demonstrated what persons with disabilities can do with any instrument. They have used theirs in the transformation and construction of Jamaican music and culture. Can you imagine what Jamaica could become if more persons with disabilities were to be provided with the technological and other support to do their work?

12

Adina Edwards:
The Queen of Gospel

The indefatigable Adina Edwards was one of the most popular female gospel artistes in Jamaica. She was blind and made her living singing gospel songs in concerts across the island.

I am weak but Thou art strong;
Jesus, keep me from all wrong;
I'll be satisfied as long
As I walk, let me walk close to Thee.

Just a closer walk with Thee,
Grant it, Jesus, is my plea,
Daily walking close to Thee,
Let it be, dear Lord, let it be.

(Kenneth Morris, Arranger 1940; recorded by Adina Edwards 1973)

This is an extract from one of the popular songs she performed when she dominated the gospel arena in Jamaica between the 1960s and the 1980s when she was known as the Queen of Gospel. Consistent attendees at concerts in that time would say, "If you want your gospel concert to be nice, just get Adina Edwards."

Edwards was born in St Andrew in 1925 and died in 2008 at the University Hospital of the West Indies (*Jamaica Observer* 2012b). In her formative years, she attended the Salvation Army School for the Blind and Visually Impaired (*Gleaner* 1974). It was there that her talent for singing was recognized and nurtured as she was encouraged to participate in various cultural activities in the city of Kingston. Soon people across the island were clamouring for her melodious singing voice at various musical events.

Edwards was a resident of Third Street in Trench Town, home of some of the most notable figures in Jamaica's music industry.

It is hard to conceive of Edwards not being involved in the music industry based on her place of birth and abode. As it stood, legendary musical figures such as Bob Marley, Bunny Wailer, and Peter Tosh all lived on First Street in the same community; Delroy Wilson was a resident on Second Street; Joe Higgs, Junior Brathwaite, Ken Boothe, and Lord Tanamo were her neighbours on Third Street; Jimmy, Desmond and Junior Tucker, Cynthia Schloss, Dean Frazer, and Ernest Ranglin all hailed from Fourth Street; Alton and Hortense Ellis, Dobby Dobson, and Noel "Scully" Simms lived on Fifth Street. On Sixth Street there were Bunny Robinson, the Techniques, and the Paragons; on and around Seventh Street were Wilfred Edwards, Toots and the Maytals, Leroy Sibbles, the Clarendonians, and Roy Shirley (*diG Jamaica* 2015). Edwards might not have been able to literally "see" these giants in Jamaica's music industry but undoubtedly their pulsating rhythms would have captivated her while the sounds reverberated in her ears. She too sought to carve out her niche in this music industry and gospel was her choice. It was a choice that reaped dividends since this genre became her sole means of economic survival.

As the mother of six children – five girls and one boy – Edwards had to fight for survival in a very competitive industry. Artistes had to be at their best to capture their audience or suffer on the sidelines. Edwards wanted to earn an honest living and the best way to do so was to use her talent. Accordingly, she depended on her melodious and captivating voice which she used to touch the lives of many persons.

The records would show that Edwards was a regular singer at the corner of King and Barry Streets in downtown Kingston – the capital city of Jamaica (*Gleaner* 2015). Equipped with her accordion, she would belt out popular gospel songs to an audience who would congregate once she started to perform. First, she would sing some of the popular church songs, thus captivating the hearts and minds of passers-by. Some of these songs included "Just A Closer Walk With Thee", "Why Don't You Write Me", "Take My Hand", and "Don't Forget To Pray". When her voice grew tired, she would reach for her accordion, her instrument of choice, on which she would play the different gospel songs while her audience sang along.

Adina Edwards was a devout Christian. This she never hid under a bushel, and one of the reasons gospel music was her chosen genre as she proclaimed the words of her Lord and Saviour, Jesus Christ.

Contextually, she always admonished her audience to pray to God for guidance and protection. Individuals who attended events where she performed said she always sang the song "Don't Forget To Pray".

While Adina sang gospel songs and played her accordion on the streets, people would give donations for her performance. This was not an ideal situation since she would have preferred to be contracted and paid for her service instead of being given an offering for her singing. But the circumstances in Jamaica at the time were such that very few people were willing to enter into employment contracts with persons with disabilities. It was not the cultural norm, the belief being that such people should be on welfare. This was the era when the welfare and medical models of disabilities were dominant. The former posited that persons with disabilities were unable to do anything for themselves and so they had to depend on the state, church or family to receive support; while the latter held that emphasis should be placed on curing the disease affecting the individual (Oliver 1990). Neither model projected persons with disabilities in a positive light, and both restricted the capacity of disabled persons to contribute to society on an equal basis with others (WHO 2011).

Nevertheless, the records show that Adina Edwards was contracted to Dynamic Sounds, the popular music label owned by iconic musician, Byron Lee, with whom she worked on a number of songs. Their relationship was short-lived, as in 1974 Dynamic Sounds terminated the contractual relationship. It was not a cordial separation and Edwards was left in a far worse position than when she had entered into the arrangement (*Gleaner* 1974).

It was while the contract was still in force that she recorded her most popular song, "Don't Forget To Remember Me". It was a cover version of one of the popular songs by the Bee Gees which she recorded and popularized in Jamaica with encouragement from popular music producer, Tommy Cowan (*Jamaica Observer* 2012).

Don't forget to remember me
And the love that used to be
I still remember you
I love you
In my heart lies a memory to tell the stars above
Don't forget to remember me my love.

(Original soundtrack from the movie, *Staying Alive*,
sung by the Bee Gees 1970; Edwards 1974).

In addition to her focus on gospel music, Adina attempted to enter the mainstream and participated in the National Popular Song Contest in 1973. While she was a local favourite, her song "Love I Festival" came second in the competition:

Jamaicans one and all
Please listen to my song
Festival time in the air again
Festival time in the air again
Come out and have some fun
Won't you come out and have some fun
Get yourself in a irie mood
Get yourself in a irie mood
Drinking whiskey and Jamaican rum.

(Edwards 1973)

Adina Edwards is remembered as one of the persons who added value to Jamaica's culture through music. In 2012 the *Jamaica Observer* did a feature on women who had contributed to Jamaica's music scene and Adina Edwards was featured among the 50 most impactful women in the industry.

More in-depth information on Adina Edwards is sparse. However, this book could not have been penned without acknowledging her contribution to Jamaica's culture through musical development. She came into this world, sang, played her accordion and touched many lives. She is saluted for her stellar contribution. She was undoubtedly a true ambassador for persons with disabilities.

Final Analysis, Conclusion and Recommendations

13

The cases presented in this book suggest a reasonable conclusion that persons with disabilities in Jamaica have contributed to the country's culture through their musical involvement – the foremost consideration in compiling these accounts. Diverse writers and scholars have chronicled the contribution of different people and sectors to the development of Jamaica's culture but none have examined the specific contributions of persons with disabilities.

It is within this context that this author has examined the works of these marginalized individuals with the aim of documenting and analysing the experience and contributions of some of these people to the cultural advancement of Jamaica through musical inclusion and participation.

With the central question being *to what extent have persons with disabilities contributed to the cultural development of Jamaica*, the specific objectives were:

- To document and show to the world that persons with disabilities have added value to the Jamaican culture through their musical contributions.
- To demonstrate that persons with disabilities have been extremely successful in their musical careers in Jamaica.
- To show that there are viable career paths in music for talented persons with disabilities.

Based on the data sources, it is clear that persons with disabilities have made a significant contribution to the development of Jamaica's culture through their involvement in manifold aspects of music and entertainment. We have seen where individuals with disabilities have been involved with the different genres of the music industry

– ska, rock-steady, roots rock reggae, gospel, dancehall, and even soca – and their rich and diverse involvement demonstrates clearly that they have a legitimate claim to their place in the development of Jamaica's culture. But in light of the challenges affecting them, this accomplishment has not been easy for members of this community. Various barriers in the Jamaican society have served to stymie the inclusion and participation of persons with disabilities in the mainstream of Jamaican society. Some of the barriers highlighted in this book are access to education, access to employment, access to public facilities, access to information, and negative attitudes and stigma. These are some of the barriers that Oliver (1990) speaks about that contribute to a disabling environment.

Notwithstanding these barriers, persons with disabilities can boast of being very successful in their cultural contribution to Jamaica. For example, as has been described in chapter 11, Fab Five has been the longest serving musical band in the island. Having been established in 1968 and having been awarded several local, regional and international awards for excellence in the music industry, members of the band have also participated in every genre of the music – demonstrating their versatility – and have travelled and played on every continent in the world, another measure of their success.

One of the contributing factors to their Herculean success is the management model they have utilized over the years. The band adopted a model that brings all its players into a central housing system, making it very easy for players to attend rehearsals and to bond together. They have also established a formula for reinvesting funds earned from multiple assignments back in the business. All of these approaches have worked very well for them and should be emulated by emerging bands.

Frankie Paul on the other hand, introduced in chapter 9, undoubtedly stamped his authority in the dance hall and became a dominant force to be reckoned with. Writing and singing over five thousand songs is no ordinary feat. It is reflective of his talent and success. In the dance hall, it was a major accomplishment for a sound system operator to have a "special" from Frankie Paul – a song that is specifically written and sung for the particular sound system. This would evoke tremendous emotional responses from people attending the dance or party. Frankie Paul has also travelled all over the world and has been a pre-eminent musical ambassador for Jamaica. He has performed in Europe, Asia, Africa, Australia, South and North America. On every continent, he has demonstrated his musical talent and shown that irrespective of having a disability, one can make a contribution to society.

Don Drummond who had his musical exploits confined to ska was extremely successful at stimulating his fans wherever the Skatalites played. He used his trombone to talk to the people who understood. As one with a mental illness, he demonstrated that you can nevertheless make a meaningful contribution to your society. His fans could not get enough of his music and there was a constant hunger for his distinctive sound in the clubs, theatres or wherever he played.

Derrick Morgan used his musical genius to entertain and thrill many Jamaicans. From the late 1950s to present, he has demonstrated an insatiable appetite for music and this appetite has been used to feed lovers of Jamaican music all over the world for over 60 years. His visual impairment has never impeded his ability to rock and cause Jamaicans to skank to his music in the dance hall, clubs and parties.

Latifa Brown demonstrated that women with disabilities have a contribution to make to Jamaica's culture through her musical and dancing exploits. Despite her physical disability, she was able to ride the rhythm and hold her own among the greats in the popular culture. Her confidence knew no bounds and she stamped her mark on the cultural landscape of Jamaica.

Adina Edwards was also very successful in the gospel genre. She transformed gospel music in the 1960s, 1970s and 1980s. She took popular hymns and other gospel songs and remixed them to her own stylized version and had fans rocking, dancing, and praising God whenever she performed.

But while most of these persons with disabilities were successful on the qualitative side of the music business, very few of them can lay any claims to being successful on the quantitative side. By quantitative side, this author is referring to the financial aspect of the business. Frankie Paul, Fab Five, and Derrick Morgan were able to show some success in this regard. However, others have pointed to numerous bad encounters with producers and managers who have robbed them of income and contributed to their failure to make money from the business. Here we see an age-old problem being raised. There are some who believe that persons with disabilities should be on welfare, and so giving them "a little thing here and there" is sufficient. This is unethical and dishonest and should be addressed with the strongest legislation for their protection.

The Way Forward

This is where the obligation of governments under the United Nations Convention on the Rights of Persons with Disabilities (CRPD) becomes relevant (United Nations 2006). It mandates States Parties to put in place legislation to protect persons with disabilities against all forms of discrimination. Article 4 states:

> States Parties undertake to ensure and promote the full realization of all human rights and fundamental freedoms for all persons with disabilities without discrimination of any kind on the basis of disability. To this end, States Parties undertake:

> a) To adopt all appropriate legislative, administrative and other measures for the implementation of the rights recognized in the present Convention;

> b) To take all appropriate measures, including legislation, to modify or abolish existing laws, regulations, customs and practices that constitute discrimination against persons with disabilities;

> c) To take into account the protection and promotion of the human rights of persons with disabilities in all policies and programmes;

> d) To refrain from engaging in any act or practice that is inconsistent with the present Convention and to ensure that public authorities and institutions act in conformity with the present Convention;

> e) To take all appropriate measures to eliminate discrimination on the basis of disability by any person, organization or private enterprise;

> f) To undertake or promote research and development of universally designed goods, services, equipment and facilities, as defined in Article 2 of the present Convention, which should require the minimum possible adaptation and the least cost to meet the specific needs of a person with disabilities, to promote their availability and use, and to promote universal design in the development of standards

and guidelines;

g) To undertake or promote research and development of, and to promote the availability and use of new technologies, including Information and Communications Technologies, mobility aids, devices and assistive technologies, suitable for persons with disabilities, giving priority to technologies at an affordable cost;

h) To provide accessible information to persons with disabilities about mobility aids, devices and assistive technologies, including new technologies, as well as other forms of assistance, support services and facilities;

i) To promote the training of professionals and staff working with persons with disabilities in the rights recognized in this Convention so as to better provide the assistance and services guaranteed by those rights (United Nations 2006: 4).

Thus far, Jamaica has established a Disabilities Act to protect persons with disabilities against discrimination and to have these individuals fully integrated into the mainstream of society. However, despite the legislation having been passed in 2014, seven years later it has not been implemented. Though it has the potential of radically transforming the lives of persons with disabilities in Jamaica, bureaucratic and political intransigence has stymied its implementation.

Efforts are being made to integrate more persons with disabilities into the mainstream educational system. This is absolutely necessary if there is to be an eradication of the social barriers that restrict the inclusion and participation of persons with disabilities which will ultimately result in sustainable empowerment and transformation of these persons (Oliver 1990). They could be trained through the education system to develop all their natural talents, including those in music.

Importantly, the negative attitudes toward persons with disabilities are some of the things being addressed by the authorities in Jamaica. However, the public education campaigns are not consistent enough. If the years of negative attitudes and stigma against persons with disabilities are to be eradicated from the Jamaican society, the public education campaigns have to be consistent and sustained (Staniland 2011; Bandura 2001).

Relatedly, musical equipment is extremely expensive and the capital outlay to start a band or sound system is prohibitive for persons with disabilities. If they do not have the musical equipment, they will not be able to participate and compete with others in the industry on an equal basis. Some support mechanism needs to be put in place to allow for these individuals to develop their skills. It is evident that music is one of the areas in which persons with disabilities can excel, and if they are given the equipment to support their talent, they undoubtedly will achieve excellence. Article 30 of the CRPD mandates that governments must put in place measures that will allow persons with disabilities to develop and hone their creative and artistic skills, not just for themselves but also to enrich the lives of others. It postulates: "States Parties shall take appropriate measures to enable persons with disabilities to have the opportunity to develop and utilize their creative, artistic and intellectual potential, not only for their own benefit, but also for the enrichment of society" (United Nations 2006: 17).

Notwithstanding the challenges confronting persons with disabilities in the music industry, this is still a viable option for persons with disabilities to demonstrate their talent. That they are excellent players of instruments has been demonstrated by Don Drummond with his trombone; Grub Cooper with his drums; Sidney Thorpe with his keyboard; and Frankie Paul on the piano. Michael Fairman has been revolutionizing the sound of modern reggae music providing proof that you can have a disability and still be competitive in the industry. Persons with disabilities are no "quacks" when it comes to the music industry, but it must expand to accommodate their inclusion and participation.

The examples presented in this work are proof that persons with disabilities have been participating and have made an impact at all levels of the society. From school to Nine-Nights; from Christians who attend gospel concerts to young people who flock the dance halls – their music has touched citizens from all walks of life. What is now required is for due recognition and commendation to be given to them for their sterling contribution to the cultural development of Jamaica arising from their musical inclusion and participation.

In this context, this author would like to recommend that:

1. the government remove taxes on any equipment that is used by

a person with disability in the pursuit of their musical career;

2. a special fund be established by the Government where persons with disabilities can get funding support to purchase equipment that they will use in their music career as a one-off contribution;

3. persons with disabilities be encouraged by government and non-governmental organizations catering to persons with disabilities to treat their musical career as a business and as such, get their business formally registered;

4. in addition to the registration process, persons with disabilities employ an honest, competent and dedicated individual who will manage the business;

5. persons with disabilities should also get training in business management skills so that they can understand what is taking place with their enterprise;

6. persons with disabilities place emphasis on consistent training to constantly improve the quality of their products; and that

7. they establish personal savings mechanisms to assist them on rainy days.

Persons with disabilities have every just reason to be proud of the stellar contribution members of their community have been making, through their musical inclusion and participation, to Jamaica's vibrant culture. We are proud to document the rich and spectacular role they have played in this area of national development. Their musical exploits have been legendary.

Afterword

SEISMIC SHIFT FOR PERSONS WITH DISABILITIES IN JAMAICA

- Contributed by the author (*The Gleaner*, Sunday, February 20, 2022).

Monday, February 14, 2022 constituted a critical juncture in Jamaica. It signalled the coming into effect of one of the most far-reaching pieces of social legislation to be implemented in the country since the Child Care and Protection Act of 1998. This legislation that was passed by the Portia Simpson Miller administration in 2014 seeks to eradicate discrimination against the estimated 450,000 persons with disabilities living in the island.

According to the Act, "discrimination" means any distinction, exclusion or restriction, on the basis of disability, which has the purpose or effect of impairing or nullifying the recognition, enjoyment or exercise, on an equal basis with others, of privileges, legal interests, rights, benefits and treatment, in the political, economic, social, cultural, civil, religious, educational or any other field, and includes all forms of discrimination, including denial of reasonable arrangements, and "discriminate" shall be construed accordingly.

Discrimination is a major socio-economic impediment against persons with disabilities. It prevents these individuals from accessing vital goods and services that would contribute to their development and inclusion in society. Resultantly, most persons with disabilities end up being isolated from education, healthcare, employment and access to public facilities. Such a situation contributes to these individuals being extremely poor as adumbrated in various global research studies.

In 2003, when I was minister of state under the P.J. Patterson administration, I set out on a journey to transform the disability landscape. In doing so, legislation was a foundational part of this journey. In this regard, special attention was placed on the negotiations that were taking place at the United Nations on the Convention on the Rights of Persons with Disabilities (CRPD) and the drafting of the Disabilities Act. The involvement of the community of persons with disabilities was instrumental to the process and I had a consultation with the leadership of the community, during which they told me that legislation, education, employment and public education relating to members of this marginalized community should be the priority of the Government.

Extensive work was done on the legislation while I was minister of state in the Ministry of Labour and Social Security. Kudos must go to two members of the technical team in the ministry at the time, Miss Netricia Miller and Mrs Carla-Ann Roper, for the Herculean support they gave in preparing the legislation.

In 2014, after I became the president of the Senate, the legislation was brought to the Parliament. It was debated and passed in the House of Representatives in July 2014 and in the Senate in October 2014. Without any hesitation, as president of the Senate then, I affixed my signature to this seminal piece of legislation. Similarly, the governor-general gave his assent in November of that year.

Taken a Long Time

Unfortunately, it has taken the Ministry of Labour and Social Security a long time to get all the necessary components such as the regulations in place to put the minister in a position to set the effective date for the legislation.

In 2020, upon assuming responsibility for the Ministry of Labour and Social Security, the Hon. Karl Samuda, in a consultative meeting with me, committed to having the Disabilities Act brought into effect during his tenure as Minister of Labour and Social Security. Thankfully, this has happened and I want to personally congratulate him for honouring this commitment. I am pledging my wholehearted support to him and the country, as well as my expertise in the implementation of the legislation as it will require knowledge and understanding for its success.

As one who has been at the forefront of preparing this legislation and advocating for its implementation, I am most elated at its coming into effect. I have a disability. I research disability and have over 20 international publications on the subject. I am a member of the United Nations Committee on the Rights of Persons with Disabilities, so I understand the value and quintessence of this legislation. My statement that it will transform the disability landscape in Jamaica is not mere cheery optimism; it is a statement of fact.

When one examines the provisions of the legislation, one will understand that it will be addressing some fundamental issues affecting persons with disabilities over the years. Discrimination is at the heart of this and the legislation frowns upon any act of discrimination against persons with disabilities. It is discrimination that has contributed to over 90 per cent of the population of persons with disabilities in the island being unemployed. It is discrimination that has caused schools to be built without accessible features for persons with disabilities, and that has placed these individuals in a perpetual state of poverty. It is discrimination that has caused only six out of the over 400 buses owned by the Jamaica Urban Transit Company (JUTC) to be accessible to persons with disabilities. And, it is discrimination that causes the vast majority of buildings in the country to be inaccessible to persons with disabilities.

Ex Ante Duty

According to the Committee on the Rights of Persons with Disabilities in its General Comments on Accessibility, accessibility is an *ex ante* duty, meaning that parties have the duty to provide accessibility before receiving an individual request to enter or use a place or service. Similarly, reasonable accommodation is viewed as an *ex nunc* duty. This means that it is enforceable from the moment an individual with an impairment needs it in a given situation. Failure to provide accessibility and reasonable accommodation/arrangement is an act of discrimination.

Now that the legislation is brought into effect, both the public and private sectors must put in place measures for accessibility and reasonable arrangements for persons with disabilities. For example, employers will have to ensure that their recruitment practices take into consideration the needs of persons with disabilities. Similarly, the Government must ensure that schools are accessible to persons with disabilities – another matter that I have been championing through the Parliament. HEART/NSTA Trust, for example, which is the national training agency with responsibility for developing and implementing policies and programmes to drive the technical and vocational education and training (TVET) system in Jamaica, must ensure that all of its institutions are accessible and inclusive of persons with disabilities.

If persons with disabilities believe that their rights have been transgressed, then they can lodge a complaint to the Jamaica Council for Persons with Disabilities (JCPD) which is now a body corporate and is mandated by law to act. The council will have to investigate the complaint and can refer the matter for mediation or send it to the Disability Rights Tribunal (DRT).

The DRT is a quasi-judicial institution that has the authority under the law to hear and make decisions on allegations of discrimination against persons with disabilities.

This legislation is going to be a game changer in jurisprudence where persons with disabilities in Jamaica are concerned. It is a results-oriented piece of legislation. I am therefore urging the permanent secretary and the minister to ensure that whosoever is hired as the executive director is someone who is a visionary and transformational leader. It must not be someone who is a profiler and just loves the video light.

The global mantra for persons with disabilities is "Nothing About Us Without Us". This means that no issue relating to persons with disabilities should be done without members of this community. Obviously, this is a strong feature of the new board of management that will govern the new JCPD. The law makes it pellucidly clear that the majority of the members of the board must be persons with disabilities or representatives of organizations representing persons with disabilities.

Citizens of Jamaica will have to play a preeminent role in the implementation of the new legislation. It is citizens who have been erecting barriers (knowingly and unknowingly) in society that limit the participation and inclusion of persons with disabilities on an equal basis with others. Thus, all these negative attitudes that citizens display against persons with disabilities will have to stop. Citizens must recognize that disability can happen to anyone. One can be fully abled today and become disabled tomorrow. We must therefore treat these individuals with the love and dignity that they truly deserve.

I really, really feel like dancing because a new day is dawning in Jamaica for persons with disabilities – a day that sets the stage for more Monica Bartleys, Sarah Newland Martins, Gloria Goffes, Henrietta Davis Wrays, Wilbert Williamses, Derrick Palmers, Arvel Grants, Conrad Harrises, and Floyd Morrises to be produced.

References

Anderson, S. 2014. *Climbing Every Mountain: Barriers, Opportunities, and Experiences of Jamaican Students with Disabilities in their Pursuit of Personal Excellence*. Kingston, Jamaica: Arawak publications.

Augustyn, H. 2013. *Don Drummond: The Genius and Tragedy of the World's Greatest Trombonist*. NC & London: McFarland & Company, Inc., Publishers.

Bandura, A. 1986. *Social Foundations of Thought and Action: A Social Cognitive Theory*. Englewood Cliffs, N.J.: Prentice-Hall.

———. 2001. "Social cognitive theory of mass communication." *Media Psychology*. (3):265-299. DOI: 10.1207/S1532785XMEP0303_03.

Berger, P.L., & P. Luckmann. 1966. *The Social Construction of Reality: A Treatise in the Sociology of Knowledge*. New York: Doubleday.

Blake, P. 1984. "Pass the tu-sheng-peng." https://www.youtube.com/results?search_query=frankie+paul+tu-sheng-peng&sp=mAEB

Blumler, J.G., & Kavanagh, D. 1999. "The third age of political communications: Influences and features." *Political Communications*. 16:209-230.

Brown, L. 2009. "Spell it out." https://www.youtube.com/watch?v=FA8XLu9jAho

Campbell, H. 2013. "Margarita, more than a dancer". http://www.jamaicaobserver.com/entertainment/margarita--more-than-a-dancer_13970203

Committee on the Rights of Persons with Disabilities. 2014. General comment no. 2 on article 9: Accessibility. https://www.ohchr.org

Cooke, M. 2016. "Miller examines Drummond and Margarita." http://jamaica-gleaner.com/article/entertainment/20160215/miller-examines-drummond-and-margarita

Cooper, C. 2004. *Sound Clash: Jamaican Dancehall Culture at Large*. New York: Palgrave Macmillan.

Crowther, N. 2007. "Nothing without us or nothing about us?" *Disability and Society*. 22(7):791–94. DOI: 10.1080/09687590701659642

diG Jamaica. 2015. "Trench Town – the birthplace of reggae." (February 23). http://www.digjamaica.com

Encyclopaedia Britannica. 2018. "Trombone-musical instrument." https://www.britannica.com

Fab Five. 1995. "Good buddy." https://www.youtube.com/watch?v =Fgm8KIX-WM4

Frankie Paul. 2011 (December 31). Interview with Angus Taylor. United Reggae. https:// unitedreggae.com/articles/n828/ 123111/ interview-frankie-paul

Gayle-Geddes, A. 2015. *Disability and Inequality: Socio-economic Imperatives and Public Policy in Jamaica*. New York: Palgrave Macmillan.

Gooden-Monteith, C. 2019. *Inclusion of Students with Special Needs in Regular Classroom: Teachers, Teachers, Knowledge, Attitude and Practice in Jamaica and Globally*. Kingston, Jamaica: Self-published.

haugustyn. 2013. "Bellevue Mental Hospital." (October 25). Blogpost. http://old.skabook.com/foundationska/2013/10/ bellevue-mental-hospital/

Higman, B.W. 2004. "History, heritage and memory in modern Jamaica." *Kunapipi*, 26(1). https://www.ro.uow.edu.au/

Hope, D. 2013. *International Reggae: Current and Future Trends in Jamaican Popular Music*. London: Pelican.

Hope, D. (ed.). 2015. *Reggae from Yaad: Traditional and Emerging Themes in Jamaican Popular Music. Selected Papers from the International Reggae Conference at the University of the West Indies, Mona Campus, Jamaica, February 2013*. Kingston, Jamaica: Ian Randle Publishers.

————. 2018. *Reggae Stories: Jamaican Musical Legends and Cultural Legacies*. Kingston, Jamaica: UWI Press.

Howard, D. 2007. "Punching for recognition: The juke box as a key instrument in the development of popular Jamaican music." *Caribbean Studies Quarterly*, 54(4):32-46. https://doi.org/10.1080 /00086495.2007.11829715

————. 2016. *The Creative Echo Chamber: Contemporary Music Production in Kingston Jamaica*. Kingston, Jamaica: Ian Randle Publishers.

Howe, B., S. Jensen-Moulton, N. Lerner, and J. Straus. (eds). 2015. *The Oxford Handbook of Music and Disability Studies*. Oxford: Oxford University Press. http://www.oxfordhandbooks.com

Israel Vibration. 1997. "There is no end." https://www.youtube.com/ watch?v=jRwSMMpGMKM

Jamaica Gleaner. 1974. https://newspaperarchive.com/kingston-glean er-mar-18-1974-p-4/

————. 2008. "Don Drummond." https://www.jamaicagleaner.com.

————. 2009. "PM reaches resolution at Gully/Gaza meeting." https://

References

www.jamaicagleaner.com

———. 2010. "Forty years of hard work: Fab 5 talk about what it took to get them where they are." https://www.jamaicagleaner.com

———. 2017a. "Latifa Brown... Strengthened by her scars." https://www.jamaicagleaner.com

———. 2017b. "$1.4m bill on Frankie Paul." https://www.jamaicagleaner.com

———. 2017c. "Frankie Paul voice gone." https://www.jamaicagleaner.com

Jamaica Observer. 2012a. "Musician Don Drummond guilty of lover's murder by way of insanity." https//www.jamaicaobserver. com

———. 2012b. "Adina Edwards – Blind gospel artist extraordinaire." https://www.jamaicaobserver.com

———. 2014. "Remembering blind gospel singer Adina Edwards." https://www.jamaicaobserver.com

———. 2016. "Frankie Paul on the mend." https://www.jamaica-observer.com

———. 2017. "Remembering Frankie Paul." (May 22). https://www.jamaicaobserver.com.

Jones, F., & L. Serieux-Lubin. 2018. *Disability, Human Rights and Public Policy in the Caribbean: A Situation Analysis*. ECLAC – Studies and Perspectives Series. Santiago: United Nations. https://www.cepal.org/en/publications/43306-disability-human-rights-and-public-policy-caribbean-situation-analysis

Katz, D. 2013. "Don Drummond: Jamaica's most talented and troubled trombonist: David Katz remembers the mercurial and majestic Skatalites member who helped lay the foundation for reggae and dancehall" (November 22) https://daily.redbullmusicacademy.com/2013/11/don-drummond-feature

Mental Health America. 2018. "Mental health and the family: Recognising warning signs and how to cope." https://www.mentalhealthamerica.org

Ministry of Labour and Social Security (MLSS). 2014. Disabilities Act 2014. https://www.mlss.gov.jm

———. 2015. *Socio-economic study on persons with disabilities in Jamaica*. Kingston: Ministry of Labour and Social Security.

Mitcham, C., & M. Ryder. 2005. "Social constructionism." Encyclopedia of Philosophy. *Encyclopedia.com*. (December 28). https://www.encyclopedia.com/humanities/encyclopedias-almanacs-transcripts-and-maps/social-constructionism

Morgan, D. 1962. "Forward march." https://www.youtube.com/watch?v=4RYaMH9WB84

Morris, F. 2017. *By Faith, Not By Sight: The Autobiography of Jamaica's First Blind Senator*. Kingston: ImagiNation Books.

———. 2020. "Accessible and inclusive city: Can Kingston Jamaica measure up?" *Disability Studies Quarterly*. 40(2). https://dsq-sds.org/issue/view/235 DOI: http://dx.doi.org/10.18061/dsq.v40i2

Murphy, X. 2005. "A conversation with Ska King, Derrick Morgan." Jamaicans.com. https://jamaicans.com/skakinginterview/

Niaah, S. (ed.) 2020. *Dancehall: A Reader on Jamaican Music and Culture*. Kingston, Jamaica: UWI Press.

Oliver, M. 1990. *The Politics of Disablement*. London: Macmillan Press.

———. 2013. "The social model of disability: Thirty years on." *Disability and Society* 28(7):1024–1026. https://doi.org.10.1080/09687599.2013.818773

Patterson, P.J. 2018. *My Political Journey*. Kingston: The University of the West Indies Press.

Prahlad, S. 2001. *Reggae Wisdom: Proverbs in Jamaican Music*. Jackson: University Press of Mississippi.

Rieser, R. 2008. *Implementing Inclusive Education: A Commonwealth Guide to Implementing Article 24 of the UN Convention on the Rights of Persons with Disabilities*. United Kingdom: Commonwealth Secretariat.

Riverfront Times. 1996. http://www.skankproductions.com/articleiv.htm

Rolling Stone. 2018. "UNESCO adds reggae to cultural heritage list." (November 29). https://www. rollingstone.com

Staniland, L. 2011. *Public Perceptions of Disabled People: Evidence from the British Social Attitudes Survey 2009*. London: Office for Disability Issues.

Stolzoff, N.C. 2002. *Wake the Town and Tell the People: Dancehall Culture in Jamaica*. Durham, NC: Duke University Press.

Straus, J.N. 2011. *Extraordinary Measures: Disability in Music*. NY: Oxford University Press.

Toots and the Maytals (featuring Terry Hall and U-Roy backed by the Skatalites). 1963. "Never grow old." https://www.youtube.com/watch?v=sOo6HdaPlFM

UNESCO. 2009. *Defining an Inclusive Education Agenda: Reflections around the 48th Session of the International Conference on Education*. UNESCO. http://www.ibe.unesco.org/sites/default/files/resources/

defining_inclusive_education_agenda_2009.pdf

———. 2017. *The Contribution of Culture to Sustainable Development.* https://www.unesco.org/

———. 2018. *The Contribution of Culture to Sustainable Development.* https://www.unesco.org/

UNICEF. 2018. *Reggae Music of Jamaica.* UNESCO: Intangible Cultural Heritage. https://www.unesco.org

UNICEF. 2018. *Report on the Situational Analysis of Children with Disabilities in Jamaica.* United Nations Children Fund. https://www.unicef.org

United Nations. 1948. *Universal Declaration of Human Rights.* United Nations. https://www.un.org/en/universal-declaration-human-rights/

———. 2006. *Convention on the Rights of Persons with Disabilities (CRPD).* UN Department of Economic and Social Affairs. https://www.un.org

———. 2018. *Disability and Development Report. Realizing the Sustainable Development Goals By, For And With Persons With Disabilities.* UN Department of Economic and Social Affairs. https://www.un.org/development/desa/disabilities/wp-content/uploads/sites/15/2018/12/UN-Flagship-Report-Disability.pdf

Vibes Kartel (produced by Askhelle). 2011. "Hold di faith." https://www.youtube.com/watch?v=7HDTlRZd5Vk

World Health Organization & The World Bank. 2011. *World Report on Disability.* https://www.who.int/disabilities/world_report/2011/report.pdf

Xavier, M. 2005. "Interview with Ska King: Derrick Morgan." https://jamaicans.com/skakinginterview/

www.ingramcontent.com/pod-product-compliance
Lightning Source LLC
Chambersburg PA
CBHW072158270326
41930CB00011B/2481